The Work of Literature in an Age of Post-Truth

The Work of
Literature in an
Age of Post-Truth

Christopher Schaberg

BLOOMSBURY ACADEMIC
NEW YORK · LONDON · OXFORD · NEW DELHI · SYDNEY

BLOOMSBURY ACADEMIC
Bloomsbury Publishing Inc
1385 Broadway, New York, NY 10018, USA

BLOOMSBURY, BLOOMSBURY ACADEMIC and the Diana logo
are trademarks of Bloomsbury Publishing Plc

First published in the United States of America 2018

Cover design: Eleanor Rose
Cover image © iStock

Bloomsbury Publishing Inc does not have any control over, or
responsibility for, any third-party websites referred to or in this book.
All internet addresses given in this book were correct at the time
of going to press. The author and publisher regret any inconvenience
caused if addresses have changed or sites have ceased to exist,
but can accept no responsibility for any such changes.

A catalog record for this book is available from the Library of Congress.

ISBN: HB: 978-1-5013-3430-6
PB: 978-1-5013-3429-0
ePDF: 978-1-5013-3432-0
eBook: 978-1-5013-3431-3

Typeset by Deanta Global Publishing Services, Chennai, India
Printed and bound in the United States of America

To find out more about our authors and books visit www.bloomsbury.com and
sign up for our newsletters.

For my students

CONTENTS

We apologists of the humanities haven't always done the best job of justifying our vocation, but it seems to me that the book is the best place for our case to make itself.

—CHRISTY WAMPOLE, "ON DISTRACTION"

Let us give the mind a new book, as one drops a lump of fish into a cage of fringed and eager sea anemones, and watch it pausing, pondering, considering its attack. Let us see what prejudices affect it; what influences tell upon it. And if the conclusion becomes in the process a little less conclusive, it may, for that very reason, approach nearer to the truth.

—VIRGINIA WOOLF, "AN ESSAY IN CRITICISM"

Prologue

A few years before writing this book, I might have celebrated the idea of arriving at an age of "post-truth." In some ways, it sounds like a fundamental goal of literary studies: how readers learn to linger in and learn from uncertainty, ambiguity, and paradox. These are fruitful things in the literature classroom—as well as for the thinker, writer, or artist more broadly. To be suspicious of truth, in this sense, is to be wary of Truth with a capital "T": definitive or absolute claims that, in truth, are more nuanced and complex, more loaded with history. Such claims to Truth are usually in the service of an interest, a very subjective vector of power that is claimed to be ahistorical, universal. Careful study of rhetoric and context often reveals claims of Truth to be riddled with contradiction or indeterminacy. So getting to a place of post-truth may have sounded like a worthwhile venture, not so long ago.

But post-truth means something more sinister these days.

"Post-truth" was designated as 2016's word of the year by the *Oxford Dictionary*. It is a concept that became vivid during the aftermath of the 2016 US presidential election, but it is something that had been creeping and building for a while. To say that we're in an age of post-truth is to suggest that this *something* has now crystalized and become glaringly apparent. This is the age when what is truthfully stated or factually reported can be dismissed as "just words"—as Donald Trump put it in his first presidential debate with Hillary Clinton. And by merely retorting that something is not true, any further inquiry is halted. Or, conversely, by claiming something patently *untrue*, one can nevertheless sow belief in such a form that floats freely away from actual life.

This is the age when grand narratives of progress are trembling at the brink, and when atavism is running rampant. It's the milieu when Friedrich Nietzsche's once-radical arguments about the slipperiness of truths and the prismatic nature of perspectives become part of mainstream thought and culture (if in garbled and often misappropriated snippets). "That's just, like, your opinion, man"—so sneered Jeff Bridges's character Jeff Lebowski in the early 1990s, in the Coen brothers' cult film *The Big Lebowski* (1998). Now those words sound less laughable, as they've been deployed on a mass scale—anyone can claim this, and not even with irony. Climate change? Rising economic inequities? Structural racism? Erosion of civil liberties? Illegal collusions? Out-of-control gun violence? That's just, like, your opinion, man.

In this atmosphere, how might literature be of help? Doesn't any work of literature—much less literary studies—open the floodgates to endless interpretation, with no firm foundations to fall back on? When stories can go viral so quickly, with ruthless efficiency—regardless of their truth-value—of what use is the slower, clumsier process of liberal arts education, in which literature and literary studies (still) struggle to thrive?

I want to say that literature is something sure to hold onto in the choppy seas of post-truth, amid the swift currents of viral news. But this is strange to say, because some of the best literature *unmoors*, even as it grips the reader. This book is about what it means to be interested in literature and what it means to teach literature at the college level, in an age of post-truth.

This book is also about the connections between literature and environment, and about writing and teaching with *place* in mind. Part of the work of literature, I want to argue, is locating firm footing in the wild rapids of this time. I'm using environmental language here deliberately, and I will return to questions of regional belonging and the aesthetics and ethics of place, throughout. While I primarily teach literature, my interests usually drift toward questions of ecology, and attunement to coexistence in ecosystems.

I put this book together while on sabbatical, up in Michigan. I was taking a year away from Loyola University New Orleans in order to finish another book (*Airportness: The Nature of Flight*), but during this time I was also reflecting on my work as a whole, and on the value and functions of what I do—in the classroom, in my office hours, on my campus, and thinking and writing in the dark of night. I was also reconnecting with the place where I grew up, a place that I love. I thought that during my sabbatical I was going to work on a book about this place, a book about Michigan—but after Trump was elected president, I felt that I had to reassess everything, and that book got pushed to the backburner (well, sort of).

How am I supposed to keep teaching—not to mention reading—literature, when the highest public office of the United States is held by a person who is utterly unbound to the words he says, or for that matter, to what he tweets? Donald Trump has been unflappable about the fact that he doesn't read books, at least not in their entirety—he doesn't have the time, apparently ("Donald Trump Doesn't Read Books"). Where does this leave books, in our cultural estimation? What is the role of literary writing in a time when widely read stories can appear (and sometimes actually *be*) far more fictional and fantastical than we could ever imagine, much less closely read in the classroom? How can literature weigh in on matters of truth, when truth has been jettisoned for something so much more entertaining—and even more persuasive?

My career up to this point has been premised on teaching college students to communicate clearly and honestly, to read widely and with savvy across literary periods and genres, and to develop a measured sense of critical awareness with respect to modern life. I believe in the importance of all these lessons. And yet, I find myself unsure of how to stand by my work—again, admittedly *slow* work—in a culture that privileges viral storytelling, constant updating of narratives (self and otherwise), and snap judgments regarding things big and small, local and global. Literature is, if anything, a slow enterprise. Whether you're a reader, a writer, or a bookseller—you are in it for a relatively long haul in terms of literature's benefits and rewards. Literature is *work*: it takes work to create, read, disseminate, and preserve. A lot of this work is abstract and often obscured from public view. Literature can feel like a very private experience—writing it, reading it, even teaching and learning it. But any way, at its most basic level—think of a required high school or college English course, early encounters with canonical texts—literature is *work*. It's to this work that I attend in the present book, unraveling my own work in relation to literature, and thinking about the broader work that literature does—and is doing, and might do—in an age of dubious connection to the written (and spoken) word.

One note here about audience. This book's essays were written with three different but overlapping audiences in mind. The first are my undergraduate students—past, present, and future—who find themselves engaged in the work of literature and may wonder what it's all about, from their professor's perspective. The second audience consists of graduate students in the humanities who are contemplating a life doing the work of literature—however unclear or amorphous that work can seem, at that stage. Then there are my colleagues and peers, others involved in the, at times humiliating, at other times invigorating, work of teaching liberal arts in an age of post-truth. These three audiences are not always easy to balance or speak to in the same way. If the tone of this book drifts and shifts, that is why.

This book—partly a collection of meditations, occasionally a manifesto, and attuned to contemporary tensions throughout—is about teaching literature, thinking about liberal arts education, and finding my place in the accelerated early twenty-first century. It's about higher education as I have experienced and thought about it over the past ten years, particularly as this time has careened dangerously into the age of "post-truth": a concept that would have fascinated and galled the late David Foster Wallace, just as it has served and continues to serve, at least for now, Donald Trump's rise to power. Where it will go from here is anyone's guess—but I want to add a book to the mix, in hope that it will find readers who likewise find themselves uncertain and entangled in the tendrils of our age.

What is literature?

It's very strange to take a full year off of doing something that you've been doing for over fifteen years, knowing that you'll return to it but are utterly detached from it in the meantime. For me, that is teaching literature at the college level. Going into sabbatical, I trusted that I would reflect on what (and how) I teach, and hopefully come up with some new ideas, maybe even some new methods.

Over the course of the year, I frequently found myself questioning the very base of what I do: what *is* literature, in the first place? In fact, this has been a nagging question for me; when I started a blog (it sounds so quaint now) in 2008, I called it "What Is Literature?" I meant this question in earnest. Even as I read more literature, taught literature classes, and wrote about literature, I was less and less sure I knew what it *was*, or what it *did*—beyond the easy definitions of poetry, fiction, and drama and their respective social functions. Because, for me, literature has also included airports, advertisements, long walks, Lego toys, and art, among myriad other things.

But even if we rein it in: what is this thing, *literature*, that seems at once so important to culture—people's stories, shared traditions, structures of meaning—and yet sometimes all too disposable, just extraneous fluff? English professors can take themselves way too seriously, and can act as if that literature is the beginning and end of all things. I don't want to fall into that trap. (Or have I already, just by writing this book?) I want to step back and think slowly and deliberately about some of the literature that has impacted my students and me—in class and beyond (I hope). I don't want to take the work of literature for granted—not in these accelerated times of general hostility to the arts and cultural diversity. But not just in these times. As I said, I've been asking this question—what is literature?—for at least ten years. And I want to keep asking it.

I find working answers in literature, often in small pieces of literature. In my classes, I often assign full novels, but we tunnel into specific passages. I think of when I teach Octavia Butler's *Dawn*, a near future, postapocalyptic alien romance that is also a metaphysical mindbender. At one point an alien is explaining to a human how he might open his mind concerning their new predicament of coexisting with the aliens, even mating with them, becoming part-them (and the aliens becoming part-human in turn). The human here has enjoyed part of this merger, but is frightened by other aspects, and their implications. But as Butler's alien Nikanj puts it:

> Interpretation. Electrochemical stimulation of certain nerves, certain parts of your brain. . . . What happened was real. Your body knows how real it was. Your interpretations were illusion. The sensations were entirely real. You can have them again—or you can have others. (189)

That first word offered by the alien is "interpretation." What more do students need to get out of an English class, really? Isn't that the work of literature, in sum: the art of interpretation? But it doesn't stop there, importantly. For Butler, interpretations are rendered as illusions, but illusions there for the weighing and choosing, and always linked to real-world conditions, sensations "entirely real." And if you read the novel you'll see that this is no simplistic dualism between mind and matter—it's all entangled, fascinatingly so.

Dawn raises troubling questions about domination, biological determination, and free will. And there is a fierce hopefulness that runs through this novel: a refusal to give up and a resistance to retreat into timeworn adages or definitions. What I love about teaching this novel is the impassioned debates that my students get into as we discuss it, concerning not just the plot of the novel but the stakes it raises: how important or unique is the human species, and how might we remain open to (maybe even *becoming*) something different, perhaps even *better*? Butler's deceptively readable fiction invites us into these quandaries, and offers no ready conclusions. *Dawn* is only the first of a trilogy on this theme, but there's something about teaching just this book that agitates endless conversation—conversation that, then, spills into the other works we read in the class. When do we *not* encounter aliens, in literature? What is literature if not an alien form that springs to life on the page?

Literature is a weird thing, and its effects can be grounding even when it unsettles things we think we know. Take a passage from Cormac McCarthy's *The Road*:

> He sat in the sand and inventoried the contents of the knapsack. The binoculars. A half pint bottle of gasoline almost full. The bottle of water. A pair of pliers. Two spoons. He set everything

out in a row. There were five small tins of food and he chose a can of sausages and one of corn and he opened these with the little army can opener and set them at the edge of the fire and they sat watching the labels char and curl. When the corn began to steam he took the cans from the fire with the pliers and they sat bent over them with their spoons, eating slowly. (73)

After reading this in class, I might ask my students to inventory their backpacks or purses, setting "everything out in a row" and taking stock of what they carry with them. We might talk about the functions of these things, how sooner or later they will use them—like the pliers and spoons that are named and then utilized mere sentences later, in McCarthy's story. We might re-view our smartphones as things among others. At the very least, we'll be off our smartphones in those moments, and in inventory mode. This can seem frivolous, or just silly. But it's part of the work of literature. It slows us down, helps us focus on the things closest to us, if, then, possibly to engage these things more thoughtfully, more respectfully.

I realize this notion of what literature can do may sound wistfully hopeful, and even utopian. But I see it happen all the time in my classrooms: my students—huddled over literature, reading and making connections, often in amazement—are connecting with each other, and with things. And this inevitably spills over the borders of the classroom and into the world beyond.

Moving bodily sideways

In New Orleans, I take regular morning walks to the Mississippi River, which flows about five blocks from my home in Uptown. I generally go to one particular spot, a big sweeping curve on the river. While technically I head to the river to fly fish, haphazardly casting an assortment of motley flies for a wide range of fish—white bass, freshwater drum, gar, needlefish—I am always struck by the variety of things I find washed up or creeping on the bank, as well as the things drifting by on the surface or swimming in the water itself. The spontaneous treasures are as much fun as the fishing.

I watch huge uprooted trees cartwheeling along, like eerie fun rides spinning by, pulled by the stiff current to be beached somewhere or washed out into the delta beyond. I see faded Doritos bags and disintegrating Styrofoam cups, tattered T-shirts and a lonely Nike Air Jordan flipped over, footless (thankfully). I like to reflect on this gnarly bank, to think about some of these river things, and sometimes to create a very partial inventory along the way. These walks offer a chance to puzzle over some of the spatial and medial spurs attached to dissimilar and seemingly random things.

To begin with then, a short list of findings from recent walks along the river bank: millipedes, a message in a bottle, butternut squash, cardboard boxes, an oil tanker, an airplane.

Mark Twain writes in *Life on the Mississippi* that the river "is always changing its habitat *bodily*—is always moving bodily *sideways*." Twain is referring to the ways that the river can move gradually, over years, across flatland—as opposed to the "prodigious jumps" of when oxbows are suddenly cutoff by a shorter direct path.

This bodily motion *sideways* also takes place on smaller scales, as the river level rises and drops on daily, weekly, and seasonally. The riverbank pulses with transitional life—with herons, wild cats, and myriad insects that move deftly in the variable space between the water and the riprap. I notice this as I am sitting on a rock tying a streamer to my line, and focusing on the mudscape beneath me, I see dozens of millipedes crawling between stones, shells, and broken glass. I think they are going after the tiny green willow and grass shoots that have shot up since the water level dropped a couple feet. I sit there transfixed by the micro-geography and these small creatures navigating it. I am eager to Google these arthropods and find out more about them, later. They run sideways into the Internet—along with most other things, these days. But in that moment, Google couldn't feel further away.

The sideways habitat of the river extends to other eccentric objects. I see a vodka bottle lodged in the wire webwork holding back the riprap; it has a piece of notebook paper inside, rolled up. A message in a bottle! What communication does it contain, what secret hides inside? I don't open it, I don't find out—in part because it has already communicated enough, by being "a message in a bottle." I assume it is an ironic message, whatever is inside: it just has that feel to it. And the river has served as a medium for this concealed yet still communicating form. The bottle's irony, its cliché, moves sideways even as it rests, closed, a visible secret, and the river flows on a few feet away, churning its chocolate murk.

Another morning, the bank is littered with butternut squash. Not just old husks with rotten pulp, but beautiful, plump, risotto-ready ripe fruits all along the river's edge. They are stunning: a still life, a miraculous bounty. I am half-tempted to take one home and have it for dinner. My friend Tom Beller, an English professor at Tulane, told me once that he has a certain fantasy of arriving home with a complete meal for his family—as if to show that abstract, scholarly work can result in real tangible rewards like food. My mind drifts sideways to Tom as I admire the squash, which by their soaked but intact labels, I can tell, had fallen off of some boat en route from Honduras. They form a wavy line, dotting the mucky bank—it is a painting, a visual haiku.

A way down the bank and across a mud flat, I see some cardboard boxes that have drifted into the shallows. They appear to be stranded, beached. They seem to be made out of industrial strength triple-walled cardboard, and they have thick blue plastic straps around them. I walk out on a telephone pole that has likewise washed into the bank and is lodged in the mud. I cannot get close to the boxes, though. The mud's sucking power is incredible, and at the end of the telephone pole (yellow poplar or *Liriodendron tulipifera*, I think), I cannot go further—my feet are instantly pulled down into a horrifyingly tacky and solid abyss. These things, the boxes, sit so close and yet are so far, inaccessible and impossible to get at, at least for me, for now, lacking telephoto lens or pirogue. All I can do is wonder about their mysterious contents, wonder if they fell accidentally off a boat or were intentionally pitched into the water, and thereby the mystery extends itself. I cannot look up these particular boxes on the Internet; I cannot scan them, or search for them on my phone. I can barely get a clear picture of them, squashed rectangular masses resting in the slough—hazy from my precarious balancing point on the pole. I make my way back to the hard-packed muddy bank, gingerly walking along on the shorn tree trunk.

A little later, a tanker churns by, pushing up a wall of water from its bulbous sub-bow and leaving a wake that disturbs the already disturbed bank. Now this is something that I can track, and I give in to the lure of the Internet: I pull up Safari on my phone and go to the site shipspotting.com, and punch in the name I see on the hull of the ship: *Eagle Torrance*. I learn that the crude oil tanker hails from Singapore, and was built in 2007 in Mihara, Japan. I glimpse a whorl of geopolitics: modes of resource extraction and logistics of transportation appear on and escape the small screen of my phone, and simultaneously the vessel travels past me, headed upriver.

Then there is a loud rent torn across the sky above me, and I look up to see an airliner banking over the river on its final descent to Louis Armstrong International Airport. This, too, is something I can access from my phone: I quickly open a new Safari window and pull up flightaware.com, and "use my location" to retrieve a radar map with live flight lines over southern Louisiana. From there, I select the AirTran flight—just by looking up I had identified the teal-colored tail and the T shape of the Boeing 717, a rather unusual model aircraft for US carriers. I see that the flight originated in Atlanta, and is one minute from touchdown here at Louis Armstrong International Airport.

I wonder how much more detail I can discover about this particular flight. I think for a moment. Perhaps someone has tweeted about this flight; I toggle over to Twitter. I search for AirTran and find their handle. But here, as in relation to the half-submerged cargo boxes, I find myself stuck, blocked. There is only one tweet: "Welcome to @AirTran. Start following us now, we'll be tweeting with you soon." The date: October 20, 2009. I'm trapped, again—not so unlike the distance between me and the cardboard boxes in the mud. More than 14,800 Twitter accounts have followed AirTran over the following years, with some hope of airfare deals or airline updates, gripes or compliments to communicate, but the airline handle is all but defunct, an aborted beginning to the promises of social media and digital networking. Meanwhile, the 717's rear engines' roar fades as the plane makes its final bank toward the airport. Little did I know then that AirTran was itself on the verge of extinction, and that exact plane about to be bought by Delta and repainted, reupholstered.

At the river's edge I am surrounded by things moving past me, and sometimes seemingly stuck. Taken together, it is a widening spiral of objects that offer enticing points of entry, even as they may lead to mere dead ends. Or at least they appear dead in the moment; many of these things are zombies, more accurately, waiting to become dislodged or take on new life.

In his long meditation on the Mississippi, Mark Twain extends his assertion to read "about" the river, and even describes the "face of the water" itself *as* a "wonderful book." Here I have followed this impulse, but I've also lingered on the weird margins of this "book," where meaning falls away, present but obscured. I like reading this book, but I also like discovering its limits, in multiple forms and elusive zones. I'm moving bodily sideways, with the river, capturing things and letting things slip through, at once.

Perspectivism and Yiyun Li's *The Vagrants*

The work of literature takes me outside as well as into realms of thought and reflection. If literary characters, scenes, and stories can lead us into other possible lives, alternative points of view, the shorthand for this might be *perspectivism*.

I recall first learning about perspectivism in a college seminar on Nietzsche and Kierkegaard. In this class, the idea of perspectivism was never a mere intellectual shrug of admittance at the impossibility of objective truth. I learned it differently, similar to how Emmanuel Alloa has described it: "Perspectivism is not a relativism, but rather the condition for a more appropriate understanding of objectivity. The more perspectives we are able to draw together, the more comprehensive our objectivity will be. Perspectivity does not *relativize*, it *realizes*" ("Post-Truth or: Why Nietzsche Is Not Responsible for Donald Trump").

But in some corners of academia right now, there is a feeling of defeat and acceptance at what is seen as an appropriation of theoretical tactics applied to regressive politics. If everyone's stories are equally valid, who is to say that Klan members cannot march, that white supremacists aren't right, just in their own way? But perspectivism, like most of what falls under the umbrella of "critical theory," isn't quite this straightforward—and for good reason.

For instance, Yiyun Li's 2009 novel *The Vagrants* is a staggering work of narrative perspectivism. The novel moves fluidly between many different characters: over the course of 300 pages, each character gradually yet steadily takes hold, and becomes an "eye" through which the reader starts to assemble a Chinese town called Muddy River. It seems to me that we need perspectivism more than ever, an openness to extra-subjective imagination that can spur empathy with respect to others.

In *The Genealogy of Morals*, Nietzsche outlined the idea as such:

All seeing is essentially perspective, and so is all knowing. The more emotions we allow to speak in a given matter, the more different eyes we can put on in order to view a given spectacle, the more complete will be our conception of it, the greater our "objectivity." (225)

Nietzsche's scare-quoted objectivity is no less than the (of course impossible) sum total of perspectives—an impossibility that balloons when one considers the vast and myriad scales of perspective possible in this world. Indeed, in *The Vagrants*, even weather patterns attain a valid perspective, one that merges with the political consciousness of the human characters: "In this period of indecision and uncertainty, old winter-weary snow began to melt. The ground became less solid, the black dirt oozing with moisture in the sunshine" (179).

The ground that becomes "less solid" in *The Vagrants* is at once the physical earth and epistemological foundations—the mindsets of those who are increasingly aware of the power struggles taking place in Muddy River during the Chinese Cultural Revolution.

The Vagrants has at least eight main characters—but that number can slide up to ten, or twelve, easily. In a quite fascinating way, Yiyun Li does not obey the logic of "main" characters: any character is likely to become an eye or a mind through which we see or understand (or not) the world of Muddy River. The novel, in other words, permeates a range of characters—major and minor, there almost is no difference in terms of serious treatment. Anyone— and one is almost tempted to say any*thing*—is potentially a real, noteworthy perspective to inhabit, whether that be for a sentence, a paragraph, a page, or across one of the broader narrative arcs of the novel. At the same time, the novel ranges over the geography of Muddy River, such that the landscape features, seasonal shifts, and animals themselves become narrative material—character vantage points, as it were. The characters—all the possible perspectives of a place—are expanded and carried out beyond limitations of age, class status, or even sentience. At one point in the novel, "Han sank into his parents' sofa; a new television set, on its beautifully crafted stand, watched him like a dark, unblinking eye" (264). Here the perspective is given a startling rotation in 180 degrees: the character Han goes from seeing to being seen, by a TV—even better, a TV turned *off*. Later, in a brief passing paragraph, we meet the carpenter and his apprentice who built the TV stand, and see inside their thoughts about the work they were commissioned to do "without more than the minimum compensation" (281). Yiyun Li thus uses perspectivism to swivel around from subjects to objects, exposing the dynamics and mechanics of the social system at hand.

The Vagrants is full of philosophical images and mind-benders, and these often make the reader pause to consider the perspectives available through the lens of narrative. Often, when the novel comments on the work of language and storytelling, these enunciations come across as the most enigmatic and unclear. Take, for instance, the character Teacher Gu, who on his way to deliver a letter to the mailbox, mumbles to someone else: "Don't ever believe in what's written down" (275).

Yiyun Li asks readers to think simultaneously about an event and its record, about how many ways an event can be seen, and how the act of retelling creates innumerable *new* points of view. *The Vagrants* does not advocate perspectivism as any kind of simple formula or positive philosophy, but rather shows perspectivism to be an inescapable condition, something to actively and consciously wrestle with. This is a condition that, when acknowledged and embraced, can lead to what Nietzsche elsewhere calls "slow reading": a decelerated mode of interpretation that keeps doors of thought open, and does not rush to easy conclusions. Yiyun Li's *The Vagrants* provides all the pleasures—as well as all the demands—of perspectival slow reading.

From Hillsdale to the swamp

"There were plenty of days coming when he could fish the swamp" (180). That line is from the end of Hemingway's "Big Two Hearted River," and in this story a swamp is a swamp is a swamp. Like perspectivism, I learned this lesson, too, in college: from a professor who refused to let us read Hemingway metaphorically—or at least, not primarily or only metaphorically, a trap so many readers and teachers fall into (the fish = ?; a bull = ?). In college I learned how to read slowly, and to take things seriously as *things*. But it was also a strange education, in some ways.

I attended a school that fancies itself as a "city on a hill." It's true that the campus is approached by roads that incline slightly upward. Trying to recall it now, seventeen years since the last time I set foot there, I can only vaguely recall these roads. They were residential lanes, interspersed with dormitories and occasional fraternity and sorority houses. The nearby town was lined with mostly shuttered businesses; a Walmart bustled a few miles beyond Main Street.

At the bottom of the hill, at the edge of a soccer field, was a swamp. I remember as a freshman looking at masses of water lilies and stands of rushes, wondering if there were bass or pike in the shallows. Having come to this college from five hours away in the northwest corner of the state, I was missing the forests and lakes I called home. But I had come here to learn.

Hillsdale College sits at an elevation of around 1,100 feet above sea level—fairly average for that part of the state. The town of Hillsdale is about twenty miles north of the Michigan/Ohio border and is surrounded by cornfields and third-growth scrub forests. The school is known for its staunchly conservative politics and its unabashed refusal of federal loans. Freshmen students tend to be reading the same things at roughly the same time. It's their own version of a Great Books program, which focuses on the Western classics: Homer, Plato, Shakespeare, Dante, Milton, Montaigne, and so on. The first few weeks of college, as I recall them, were grueling: a heavy reading load piled on top of all the unacknowledged stresses of meeting new people, making friends, falling madly in love with various people over the course of days, and generally figuring out who I was in this new place. I had prepared for a cohort of like-minded college goers, tackling the big questions of existence. I hadn't anticipated all the smaller questions swirling around this new social scene that would make my heavy Norton anthology seem irrelevant.

Attempting to find my identity here, I tried a few things. Not knowing what I was in for, I went to a Young Life rally and was quickly weirded out by the Christian rock and the euphoric looks on the faces of the students in attendance who waved their hands in the air. Another day, after dinner in the cafeteria, I found myself suddenly crammed into a Buick with a few others, and we joined a caravan of vehicles headed to Battle Creek, where Newt Gingrich was scheduled to speak. After a half-hour of waiting, Gingrich barreled out onto a stage and launched into nonsensical invective; and then, just as fast, he shuffled off the stage and headed off for another venue. The audience roared and applauded hysterically. This was the fall of 1996, and a contingent of conservatives were freaking out at the prospect of another four years of Bill Clinton. (Some still have not gotten over these times.) Enthusiasm notwithstanding, the College Republicans and Young Conservatives were not for me. A few weeks later, I went rock climbing with a Libertarian at a cliff on the Grand River, outside of Lansing. But there was something slightly unnerving about trusting someone to hold your belay line when they are concurrently pontificating about the virtues of selfishness.

My first roommate, Lars, came from Norway. He was great, and what an experience: to spend my first semester of college with an international student. Unfortunately, Lars was completely put off by the school's rigid politics, and he headed home to Scandinavia within the first two months. My next roommate was a nice enough guy, but our room became a parade of friends at all hours, Doritos and Cheetos littering the pale blue industrial carpet. The whiny refrains of the Dave Matthews Band looped incessantly, rebounding between open doors, up and down the dormitory hall. I spent as much time as I could away from my dorm. I made friends with a few women who invited me to spend time in their dorm's common room, where we'd watch television shows with books cracked on our laps, flirtation commingling with spectation. Probably not the most effective studying technique, but it got me through many an evening.

I eventually found something that made me feel at ease: I started to sleep under a white pine on the college campus, in a grove of trees outside the library. My sleeping bag still held the faint scents of the north woods, and the white pine needles that made my bed echoed this aroma. This spot was just off the patrol path of campus security, and a world away from the awkward dynamics of the dorm rooms and the cigarette smoke-filled student union. Here, I found some quiet—if not yet myself.

Most of our classes were small, with fewer than twenty students. Several were discussion oriented, with students and professor sitting in a circle, exchanging ideas. In a cruel turn of fate, one of the only larger, lecture-style courses I had at Hillsdale was a biology course entitled "Conservation." The class took place in a narrow, amphitheater-shaped room that seated probably 100 students in total. It was one of the few "soft science" courses that still satisfied our science requirement. In a second cruel turn of fate, the course was held at 8:00 a.m. The class was full of slumbering athletes and seething economics majors. The poor professor (I can't even recall his name) lectured on the history of conservation movements and environmental protection in the United States. The lessons brimmed with dates, abstract units, and watered down explanations of pollution levels. The course was one of the driest academic experiences of my four years at Hillsdale. This was tragic, really, as it was also the topic that was arguably the most important.

Hillsdale College really catered to three different (and sometimes overlapping) demographics. There were the evangelical Christian students, who came from all over the country and were often sent by parents who wanted to protect their children from the immoral morass of normal US college campuses. Then there were the students who came to Hillsdale to seriously study Austrian economics and immerse themselves in conservative intellectual traditions—and who often had business or politics in mind. The final group of students had ended up at Hillsdale either on a sports scholarship or because it was the school that offered them the best financial aid package; there are dozens of small liberal arts colleges throughout the Midwest, and many high school students simply cast a wide net and see what comes back. The point being, not all students at Hillsdale were there for the school's explicit mission—and even those that were were cumbersomely divided between the economically minded and the religiously fervent, uncomfortable ideological step-cousins at best.

Another biology course I took at Hillsdale was much more rewarding. It was an upper-level course called "Michigan Flora," and it was taught by the improbably named Dr. Crabtree. There were two students in the course: me and a woman a year ahead of me who was gorgeous, independent, and whip smart. I always wondered how she ended up at Hillsdale, but I was too shy to move beyond catkins and drupes. When the snow thawed and the ground warmed, we spent some of our class hours cruising around the county in a big white Oldsmobile station wagon with Hillsdale's logo on the doors, looking for various wildflowers and brambles in the fecund ditches along the roadside. Along one dirt lane with driveways meandering off to dodgy abodes, Dr. Crabtree told us to look out for stray cannabis plants along the roadside: "We could make an extra few bucks." The final exam for the course consisted of 200 buds, seeds, and seedpods meticulously arranged on the lab tables; we had to identify them all. I think I managed to pull off a

B+ in the course, and I had to work for every single point—there was no room for interpretation in that class.

Wading through these memories of my years at Hillsdale proved trickier than I anticipated. The one-sentence version of this personal history has always been easy: I spent four years at a small liberal arts college in southern Michigan, and graduated with degrees in English and Philosophy. But as soon as I attempt to transport myself back to this place in my mind, when I try to retrace my steps on the ground, as it were, it all gets strange—slow and murky. All sorts of brief glimpses and minor anecdotes turn into tangles of branching sub-stories, interactive evasions, and looming embarrassments. Memory is a squishy place—seemingly clear from a distance but easy to get lost in if you plunge into it. Sort of like a swamp.

Wandering around this place again in my mind, I realized gradually that there were a lot of things I didn't really want to remember. For each friendship that blossomed, there were several aborted attempts at connecting. For every quirky adventure or playful caper, there were countless mundane experiences that wish to remain muddy and uncataloged. They sink back in just as abruptly as they appear for an instant. I'm uncomfortably aware of an urge to romanticize certain scenes from my college years, while dynamically suppressing or submerging so many others. Yet this, too, is part of the story I'm trying to tell, as it relates to the work of literature in an age of post-truth. I can say with confidence that I received a very good education at Hillsdale, in spite of (or perhaps even due to) the school's oddities. Still, certain events and epiphanies—both in the classroom and outside—seep down and elude my grasp.

Here's something that really happened, though: I took what I learned in that Michigan Flora course back home with me the following summer, and I rediscovered the woods and dunescapes that I knew by heart if not yet by head. I saw everything anew that summer: the ingenious technics of basswood seed dispersal; the cinnamon ferns that sent up gnarled seed stalks so dissimilar from their otherwise lush foliage; the brilliant cardinal lobelia that appear in late summer, their bright red flowers ridiculously luminous against the muted browns and greens that dominate the cedar swamps; the alien form of Jack in the Pulpit, a devout figure that couldn't have been further from the pews from which my Christian classmates prayed to be saved.

Still this newly discovered form of knowledge can only get one so far. To this day, I occasionally get lost in the swamps between my parents' home in the hills and Lake Michigan, a quarter-mile away. It's difficult to describe the disorientation that can occur within the implausible darkness of thick cedar stands, with their webwork of branches and wild grape vines as thick as human arms snaking up into the upper canopies of massive white pines that blot the sun's rays. It is a veritable labyrinth with living walls and vertiginous depths, both vertical and horizontal. The spongy ground has an eerie feel beneath one's feet, the result of the cedar trees' wide but shallow root structures allowing springs and streams to flow literally right beneath the trees. Sometimes a spring can be seen burbling up out of the ground, crystal clear water undulating up from a seemingly depthless reserve. Occasional northern red oaks, foliage floating far above the cedars and pines, block out the daylight and make confident orientation all but impossible.

Hillsdale College taught me to know swamps by the diversity of their life forms—this was scientific knowledge, but it also led unwittingly to a more profound sort of respect for these ecosystems. The hours and days I've spent roaming the swamps near my home in northern Michigan have given me an intense, intimate understanding of these landscapes; these are places I seek out whenever I need to clear my head, take some deep breaths, and maybe even get lost.

When I first heard Donald Trump's "drain the swamp" slogan, I remember being struck not just by the implicit hypocrisy—someone with vast wealth and a branded empire to protect hardly has any incentive to do away with special interest groups and lobbyists—but also because it sounded like ecocide. The expression clearly draws on the common (if misguided) sense of swamps as waste spaces: unnavigable, gloomy, and all but impossible to build on. But as my colleague Hillary Eklund, who has studied extensively soil science in the early modern period, pithily explained in an email to me, "swamps are the lungs of the planet." Drain them, and we might as well kiss the earth as we know it goodbye.

This sentiment was corroborated by my friend Jon Bonkoski, a Geographic Information System technician for EcoTrust who specializes in watersheds. When I asked him about the challenges and important lessons involved in mapping swamps, Jon noted: "delineating the extent of a wetland is hard due its ephemeral nature. The bigger picture, however, is the actual value of wetlands.

They are amazing and play hugely important roles in the lifecycles of many species, especially fish and insects." Such a big picture is exactly what I feel out in the cedar swamps in Michigan, where bobcats slink through the delicate maidenhair ferns; where pileated woodpeckers methodically make rectangular holes in the tree trunks; where bullfrogs crouch and converse in the peat; and where kingfishers dart along the banks of the deeper pools. One of my favorite fly-fishing locations is in this swamp, a beaver pond that boasts a remarkable diversity of fish species for a body of water not much bigger than the swimming pool at Mar-a-Lago. When I'm in this teeming place, encompassed by and enmeshed with the living, breathing environment, the phrase "drain the swamp" makes me shudder all the more.

Of course Trump's statement was never meant to be taken literally. But nevertheless, as a literature professor I cannot help but linger on the choice of words, on the implications of this metaphor. This is why I had contacted my colleague about the slogan: partly to see how it squared with science, and partly to see what the expression concealed. As Hillary went on to remark in her email to me, "swamps have always been caught up in a weird tug between desire and disgust and Trump's eagerness to get in there and 'drain the swamp' says as much about his desires for material and personal advancement as it does about his desire to correct something that has apparently gone wrong." It becomes an anxious contradiction, then, to pledge to drain the very ground while simultaneously promising to make the nation sitting on top of it "great again."

One October morning of my senior year, there was an odd energy abuzz throughout the campus buildings. Professors huddled in the halls, whispering; some of my female classmates were crying. The news gradually leaked out: the college president's daughter-in-law, who worked in a publicity capacity for Hillsdale, had committed suicide in a gazebo in the campus arboretum, in clear view of one of the women's dormitories and adjacent to the swamp at the bottom of the hill. Her death was followed by a torrent of rumors concerning her illicit romantic involvement with her father-in-law: the very president who had penned multiple books about Christian values and conservative moral imperatives, and who had brought the college into its zenith as a redoubt of traditional Western values. Within days the president had vanished. There was hardly a mention of what had taken place—no public forum or discussion groups about how we were to process this breach of everything we'd been taught. The gazebo was power-washed, whatever residual traces of blood and brain that remained running off into the fen at the edge of the carefully curated collection of trees and flowering shrubs.

By the time I graduated the following spring, Larry Arnn had been appointed as the new president of Hillsdale. Graduation day went without a hitch; I shook the new president's hand for the first time, as I received my diploma. The next morning, I paid one last visit to the white pine I used to sleep beneath. As I drove out of town in my hand-me-down Volkswagen Jetta, stuffed with all my earthly belongings and headed for the mountains and rivers of the American West, I felt the wetlands surrounding Hillsdale simmering in the sweltering humidity of a burgeoning Midwest late spring day.

As I look back on my time at Hillsdale, I register how it tuned me into both literature and landscape, always entwined. To this day, the swamp remains at the edge of the Hillsdale campus, an object correlative of the inescapable realities of life on earth: the complex networks that make human progress (as well as our missteps) possible in the first place. Nothing to simply drain or merely metaphor away, the swamp both stands for and is a vital reminder of the importance of our delicate, intricate ecosystems—and our equally tenuous place in them.

Teaching at the end of the world

Whenever the weather is even minimally conducive in New Orleans, I take my classes outside and we sit in a circle to discuss the day's reading. I keep lobbying our university administration to construct some elegant seating emplacements around our campus that could be utilized on such occasions, but to no avail (at least not yet).

So we bivouac on a piece of sunbaked swamp sod, half-shaded by a live oak for those who overheat easily, and we pull out our copies of *Robinson Crusoe* or *Frankenstein*, *Tender Buttons* or *White Noise*, and a student invariably will ask, "Why is the ground always wet?" Well, because we're under water, basically. That's why when an oil tanker churns by, headed upriver, you find yourself looking *up* to see it: the Mississippi River is actually *above us*. It's also in part why the fire ants are vigorously, ceaselessly building up their dirt mounds: to achieve a modicum of firm terrain on this eroding edge of the continent. Interestingly, you won't find much under "ecology" if you research the fire ant on Wikipedia on your smartphone. Perhaps it hits too close to home. Yes, the delta is vanishing at a rate of a football field each hour. No, I don't know how long that gives us here. Let's open to page 36, and think about how our novel is founded on the non-simple space of the beach.

Louis Armstrong International Airport is the second lowest airport in the world, at about four feet above sea level. (Only Amsterdam's Schiphol Airport is lower, at eleven feet below sea level.) The city of New Orleans is currently in the midst of constructing of a brand new, state-of-the-art, "world-class" airport terminal—aspiring to become at least a small-scale "aerotropolis." How am I supposed to incorporate this building project, this mirage of progress, into my teaching and research? Will this space stand simply as a shimmering and seamless transition zone for new students arriving each fall semester? Will the new airport be unquestionable, an utterly straightforward social text? Will our baggage arrive bathed in a sublime aura, at last? Will the air be safe from contaminants, diseases, and other pollutants? Or will the new control tower stand like Ozymandias, an object lesson for a poetics of the brazen?

Sometimes it seems like the most important thing I can do these days in my classes is to preserve a space for slow reading: seventy-five minutes, two times a week, where we can sit or crouch—be beached—on sinking ground, and read words on pages, to think about these words together, how narrative congeals (or not), how images snap into focus (or get weird), if only then to find ourselves in the world, the actual world with all its consequences. To rephrase a line from the preface of Nietzsche's *Daybreak*, at present it is not only my habit, but even my taste—a perverted taste, maybe—to teach nothing but what will drive to despair everyone who is "in a hurry." Slowness—it seems to me that this is one of the truly inestimable skills, maybe even a form of art, that I can model to my students, and even teach them how to do it: how to decelerate before meaning, to not rush to judgment or opinion. Yet how do I balance this desire with or measure it against the simultaneous urgency of ecological awareness, not to mention social justice?

I worry that I am regressing. A major highpoint of my time teaching at Loyola University New Orleans happened one November, when I joined my colleague David White from the biological sciences, who takes about thirty students out with him each fall on an evening canoe trip in the bayous surrounding New Orleans. The students get a crash course in "landscape ecology," or the multiple mosaics of relationships and processes taking place across given ecosystems, at various scales. The trip included several floating stops to discuss the invasive and prolific *Triadica sebifera* (Chinese tallow or popcorn tree), the water hyacinths spinning by, the channels dredged by humans a century ago—in short, the objects and animacies of this fragile if fecund riparian system. By the end of this evening on the water, the students seemed enchanted—if also perhaps a little exhausted. I had watched them slow down, pay attention, listen. David took extra care to draw attention to the quietude, the sounds of the bayou away from the highway we'd arrived on.

But I digress. I was talking about regression. Ever since that night on the bayou, or maybe it started before, I've found myself wanting to get back to teaching nature writing, that arguably naïve genre, that earnest kind of literature that strives contradictorily for "contact, contact!" in Thoreau's words. What is happening to me? I've read my eco-criticism carefully, I know my high theory, I wrestle with the Derridean aporia of "nature as self-proximity"—why do I want to linger with my students in literary representations of nature, simulacral ecologies as they are? What are these paradoxical pleasures, being *in* nature and learning to see it (as if "it" even exists!) in literature? The work of literature increasingly finds me longing for place—stable, grounded place—and to linger there with my students.

As we paddled back to the vans, through pitch-black night, an eerie spotlight darted erratically up ahead, piercing the skein of cypress trees and Spanish moss. A low rumble and sputter echoed across the water. It was hard to make out what it was that was approaching us, but gradually it, or rather *they*, appeared: Cajuns, a bunch of them, a gaggle of friends or maybe a family, piled into an unbelievably clamorous boat—if you could call it that. It was a mishmash splashing craft weighed down with all sorts of things, chugging through the black night aiming a military grade spotlight, looking for alligators (or so David thought). This was a strange moment, we gliding by in our canoes and college sweatshirts, and they in camouflage jackets rumbling past, blasting us with pivot-mounted incandescence. No words were exchanged, not out of tension or spite but merely due to the noise of their gurgling motor.

Maybe I believe, channeling Nietzsche once more, that reading nature writing itself, perhaps, will not "get things done" so hurriedly:

but it will teach how to read *well*: that is, slowly, profoundly, attentively, prudently, with inner thoughts, with mental doors ajar, with delicate fingers and eyes. This is my regression, and I'm afraid it's not going away anytime soon.

Starting again with Twentieth-Century American Fiction

Twentieth-Century American Fiction: this is the course my doctoral work most clearly prepared me to teach, and which I've taught regularly for many years at Loyola. The way I teach it, it's reading heavy, about a novel per week with short stories interspersed occasionally between. The exams are brutal, but my students seem to relish them: two pages of tricky passage identifications that, together, can form a sort of argument or snapshot of the arc of the class. The students write furiously for seventy-five minutes, and leave the classroom shaking out their fingers from extensive pen-clutching. It's the sort of classic college assignment that feels at once very old fashioned yet incredibly rewarding for us all: it is the experience of knowledge-creation in action, and I cherish the looks on my students' faces as they turn in their exams when I can tell that they know they've written well, connecting the dots and putting keywords and concepts to work. This makes the work of literature sound so precious, but in the hyper-profusion of screens and media feeds, it is something to behold and something to maintain.

Coming back to teach again after a year away, and now that we've entered (at least officially) the age of post-truth, I feel compelled to rethink the whole class. After all, the last century of conflicting American narratives got us to where we are now—this crazy time stretched between rabid isolationism and nationalism on the one hand, and progressive, globally minded disbelief on the other. How did we get here? And what might the texts I normally teach have to say about this moment?

After the election of Trump, I started having small-scale crises about what to teach, how to teach, and basically what it's all for, especially as it relates to this bread-and-butter course, which is usually packed: our literature students and creative writers usually want to bone up on the narrative traditions that have shaped—and spill right into—our current moment. While it's called "Twentieth-Century American Fiction," it was clearly called this back when we were *in* the twentieth century. I take the class from the turn of the twentieth century right up to the present, often ending the class with texts I've just read or even have yet to read, when I assign them, and I read these texts for the first time alongside my students. The point, in my mind, is to get students to connect dots from tensions and pressures over 100 years ago, to see where we are now (if not exactly to see it all crystal clearly, neatly causally, or see a way out of it).

Over the past eight years, I've organized the course around various themes. I called one iteration of it "Bad Romance" and we started with Lady Gaga's song and music video, which we come back to again and again throughout the semester as we read different American narratives of love and loss. Another version of the class focused on frontiers, borders, and transgressions. I tend to mix up the core readings each time I teach the course, but I have some that have remained on the syllabus from year to year. As I rethink this course now that a new political regime is at hand—a regime that is poised to dramatically rewrite (if not outright obliterate) American history—I want to mull over some of the key texts I like to teach, and think about what they have to say, now.

I often begin class with Kate Chopin's "The Story of an Hour." This very short story—just over 1,000 words—nicely exemplifies how American Romanticism slides into Naturalism around the turn of the century. Consider this passage:

> She could see in the open square before her house the tops of trees that were all aquiver with the new spring life. The delicious breath of rain was in the air. In the street below a peddler was crying his wares. The notes of a distant song which some one was singing reached her faintly, and countless sparrows were twittering in the eaves. (352)

In this scene, our narrator Louise Mallard, gazing out her upstairs window, takes in a hopeful, synesthetic overload. She is on the brink of unbound freedom, and this is reflected in the rush of sensations in the perceptual frame. But, contra the Romantic wish image, here a single human's individual will is not enough to capture this moment; the hope conveyed in this passage catastrophically falls apart by the close of the story. It occurs to me now that it also is a story of a glass ceiling *almost* shattered—so close, but not in the end. The story is undone by "alternative facts"—a misreported news item—while the sparrows promise to twitter anew, if always indifferently, long after the story ends. I think I'll keep this text as the jumping off point for my class.

Often the second text we read is Sarah Orne Jewett's "Bold Words at the Bridge." This story offers a concise case study for demonstrating how Naturalism can be inflected by Regionalism: how the lure of a stable "place" with discrete boundaries and knowable inhabitants can nevertheless result in a situation of disconnected beings and cruel geography. The story centers on a squabble between longtime neighbors:

> The two small white houses stood close together, with their little gardens behind them. The road was just in front, and led down to a stone bridge which crossed the river to the busy manufacturing village beyond. The air was fresh and cool at that early hour, the wind had changed after a season of dry, hot weather; it was just the morning for a good bit of gossip with a neighbor, but summer was almost done, and the friends were not reconciled. (121)

Notice how the quaint cottages "with their little gardens" are set against "the busy manufacturing village beyond." This story abounds with such subtle yet strong contrasts and oppositions: town and country, public and private, human and animal, animal and plant, native and foreigner, and so on. Tensions between these oppositional figures play out through the story, unsettling any easy sense of which side is, or should be considered, primary. It is a deceptively simple story, but "Bold Words at the Bridge" is an impressively compressed tale of border disputes, immigrant culture, and the contested meanings of home. So, yes, this story too is a good candidate for remaining on my syllabus.

The first full book we read in the class is Gertrude Stein's *Three Lives*. This book is difficult to categorize. Is it three stories? Or two novellas and a short story? Or a novel? Something else altogether? Whatever it is, it's an amalgam of three women's lives in the same region around the turn of the twentieth century: the ever-scolding but somehow "good" Anna, the "wandering" Melanctha, and the gentle Lena. The shared geography is a ruse. The characters never cross paths, though they intersect one another thematically in their shared hardships, if not their direct lines of existence. The book draws together threads of Naturalism and Regionalism but introduces stylistic innovations that we associate with Modernism. Many of the paragraphs read more like de-familiarizing poetry than straight up storytelling. And the stories plots, when analyzed carefully, are weirdly staggered in time and place, shaped by fractal patterns of description and narration rather than clean linear arcs. But I'm not sure if I can justify spending a whole week on this text, again. Its brutal tales of immigrant (by different means) women and their bleak fates in the early-twentieth-century United States seem almost too much to bear—and too tempting to see as anticipatory of this age of sneering-masculinist power and corresponding clampdowns. Don't get me wrong, I love this book; Stein's way with prose is unsettling in the best way. Thinking this through here, perhaps the difficulty of this book, including its depressing prescience, is precisely the reason to continue to teach it. If its repetitions are infuriating and its racial stereotypes are offensive, all the better to show students the relentlessness of certain ideological insistencies—if then to begin to dismantle them just as relentlessly.

I'm only three texts into this reflection—with too many to go—if I am to keep my short chapter format. This is going to take longer than I expected, but I feel that I should persevere. After all, when I have ever taken the time to think through an entire course, piece by piece, and explore (and sometimes justify, and sometimes reject) what it is that I am doing? I said that this is what I was going to spend my sabbatical doing: reassessing my teaching offerings. I'll press onward. This kind of staying with something difficult is part of my resistance to the haphazard speed of this age of post-truth.

Something misplaced

Or maybe I've just been delaying talking about Ernest Hemingway. As an English professor, and as someone from Michigan, Hemingway is such an annoying specter: his name is always among the first that people cite when they hear the word "literature," or if you are a writer—and this only gets worse when the state of Michigan is invoked nearby.

In my Twentieth-Century American Fiction course, I have almost always taught *The Sun Also Rises*, which I find to be a sardonic and yet weirdly moving novel. No, I didn't just "find" the book to be this way: I was taught it, at Hillsdale, by my professor Pete Olson. Later, at University of California, Davis, I was the teaching assistant for a summer course on Hemingway, taught by Peter Hays. By the time I received my PhD I had probably read the novel six or seven times. And then teaching it myself, in my own way, year after year, deepened my love of this novel—even despite the irritating aspects of Hemingway's legend and lore. *The Sun Also Rises* offers so many scenes that can be read carefully and slowly in class so as to crystalize various lessons of American Modernism (even though it takes place entirely in France and Spain). Its understatement, use of irony, meta-fiction (some of the characters—except the narrator, ironically—are struggling novelists), war-torn consciousness, and imagism, these things are all hallmarks of what makes this ambiguous period (or aesthetic movement) congeal. If Stein's *Three Lives* explores the misery of domestic labor on an American coast, then Hemingway's novel plumbs the depths of American privileged psyches gallivanting homelessly abroad.

But I don't think I'll assign *The Sun Also Rises* next time I teach the course. Instead, I'm leaning toward assigning Hemingway's story "Up in Michigan"—which is, to put it bluntly, a sickening rape story. Yet it sticks closer to the "American Fiction" designation of the course; it will let us revisit themes of women's oppression and the entrapments of Regionalism; and it will let me dedicate a full book to another author—someone not as insistently canonical as Hemingway is supposed to be.

Continuing along the path of Modernism, we also read some F. Scott Fitzgerald. I've taught a few different Fitzgerald texts in this class, a couple short stories and once the unfinished novel *The Last Tycoon*. But given its framing device involving air travel and its mixture of hilarity and sadness, I will stick with "Three Hours between Planes": a story about identity confusion and nostalgia that seems somehow appropriate for understanding how the message "Make America Great Again" was expected to arrive on a gilded jetliner some seventy-seven years hence. Against all odds, Donald Trump tapped into some wild nostalgic fantasy, and many US voters imagined in him a sort of incredible Jay Gatsby figure that they could believe in—of course, Gatsby is revealed to be something of a fake. Here's how another of Fitzgerald's similar characters, Monroe Stahr, is described in *The Last Tycoon*:

> He had flown up very high to see, on strong wings when he was young. And while he was up there he had looked down on all the kingdoms, with the kind of eyes that can stare straight into the sun. Beating his wings tenaciously—finally frantically—and keeping on beating them he had stayed up there longer than most of us, and then, remembering all he had seen from this great height of how things were, he had settled gradually to earth.

Isn't this something like how Trump is envisioned, by many? As someone who has a kind of crystal clear, total vision—achieved from high above but somehow rooted "to earth"? And isn't it the case that people see in Trump, an individual earned this god's eye view by "beating his [own] wings tenaciously" (if often visibly "frantically"), and that this illusion of self-reliance is key to his success? Critical to most of Fitzgerald's male protagonists, however, is their inescapably tragic nature. Gatsby's demise is almost anticlimactic at the end of Nick Carraway's truly whacky, 47,000-word tornadic recounting. Stahr's romantic film producer is derailed by a vision from the past and plagued by imminent heart failure. Donald Plant, in "Three Hours between Planes," is another strong male red herring of sorts: a blundering victim of modernity, including the false promises of aerial transit and the foils of romance in an accelerated communications age (the telephone and the airplane are coconspirators, in this story). If we cannot yet see Trump as a thoroughly tragic figure being sucked into the whirlpool of history, Fitzgerald's scions offer pretty convincing blueprints for how this is likely to end up.

If I'm not going to teach a Hemingway or a Fitzgerald novel, this means the second full book in the class could become Ralph Ellison's *Invisible Man*; or, if I want to push students think more about the flexible formal possibilities of fiction, I might choose Jean Toomer's hybrid masterpiece *Cane*. Or, perhaps I've made room for both of these books in the class—although *Invisible Man* is a bit longer than I like to ask students to read (closely, carefully, slowly) in a week. In both of these novels we can move away from the as-if total whiteness of American fiction, and discuss African-American traditions and struggles as they played out in the new American century. Here is an imagistic moment from *Cane*:

We were sitting on a flat projecting rock they give the name of
Lover's Leap. Some one is supposed to have jumped off it. The
river is about six hundred feet beneath. A railroad track runs up
the valley and curves out of sight where part of the mountain
rock had to be blasted away to make room for it. The engines of
this valley have a whistle, the echoes of which sound like iterated
gasps and sobs. (60)

Note how the Romantic vista immediately gives way to a suicidal
plunge. Likewise, the meandering river at the bottom of a canyon
gives way to an industrial railroad track, the mountain which "had
to be blasted" to accommodate human progress. And yet, when the
train engines whistle here, the effects are of sorrow and suffocation.
Toomer's kaleidoscopic, mixed perspectives help achieve such
a critique of American modernity as it yet charges forth into the
middle of the century.

Speaking of hurtling forward, Flannery O'Connor's story "A
Good Man Is Hard to Find" comes next, a road-trip story doomed
from the first line: "The grandmother didn't want to go to Florida"
(1). This story could serve as an ethnography of the origins of
Trumpism: rampant paranoia about the ill-intent of others, which
becomes a self-fulfilling prophesy of sorts.

About midway through the semester, my students will sometimes
complain that my course is a real downer. It is, at least at surface level,
a catalog of failed attempts at grasping love, adventure, pleasure,
escape, self-actualization, and greatness: but always ending in failure.
I don't plan it this way, I exclaim—it's just what is in the archive, it
is what makes up American fiction when we read it carefully! But I
should really rename the class "U.S. fiction," instead of "American
fiction": the course is about the United States and its attendant
fantasies, and to call it "American" is to risk eliding the fictive
landscapes of the rich, textured regions to the north and to the south.
This renaming is something I will do when I teach the class next.

But as a counterargument to this renaming, James Baldwin's
Giovanni's Room complicates things. A sort of retelling of *The
Sun Also Rises*, Baldwin's David discovers intimacy and maybe
even love in Paris—but a deep-seated self-loathing keeps him from
finding his equilibrium. Much of the novel takes place figuratively
"underwater"—the narrative is littered with aquatic language—
perhaps for this reason. At one point David muses, "Perhaps, as we
say in America, I wanted to find myself. This is an interesting phrase,

not current as far as I know in the language of any other people, which certainly does not mean what it says but betrays a nagging suspicion that something has been misplaced" (21). Something misplaced: this notion or hunch haunts the archive, and reappears even when things seem the most deliberately *in place*.

This thread could be followed through the entirety of Vladimir Nabokov's *Lolita*, a novel that is enthralling to teach and equally challenging to convince students of its merit, what with its pedophilic (reductive but accurate) protagonist Humbert Humbert. There's always the moment in my classes when the students react with horror at just how *old* Humbert is, compared to Lo. I recall the year that I registered his *old age* as exactly the year I had just turned. I told my students that I was the same age as Humbert, and they looked at me in shock, as if I were admitting by proxy other affinities to HH.

Interwoven with the more glaring examples of Humbert's perversions and perspectival loop-d-loops, other poignant observations appear, like this ruthless critique of Americana:

> Not for the first time, and not for the last, had I stared in such dull discomfort of mind at those stationary trivialities that look almost surprised, like staring rustics, to find themselves in the stranded traveller's field of vision: that green garbage can, those very black, very whitewalled tires for sale, those bright cans of motor oil, that red icebox with assorted drinks, the four, five, seven discarded bottles within the incompleted crossword puzzle of their wooden cells, that bug patiently walking up the inside window of the office. (211)

The "stationary trivialities" that comprise consumer culture find themselves to be the things misplaced—as if, once invented and disseminated, their human custodians have forgotten what it means to care for things. All the objects for sale are juxtaposed with "that bug patiently walking up the inside of the window": look how the living creature, AKA nature, ends up inside the gas station, once more displacing the scene and leaving us spinning as to who or what here should be granted priority. This kind of ontological uncertainty, spoon-fed to us by an uncertain subject par excellence—HH—makes *Lolita* a key text for Twentieth-Century American Fiction. Even as it seems to get more uncomfortable to teach this novel with each year, I can't imagine taking it off the syllabus. Then it would really feel like something had been misplaced.

I could keep going with this inventory qua analysis of the texts for this class, but I think it will be better to spread them out less formulaically across subsequent chapters. Just going this far through the readings has reaffirmed my commitment to the course, and anyway I'd hate for it to end up seeming like a mere inventory of texts, a checklist to simply mark off, or a shopping list of sorts. If college curricula follow a consumerist logic, let it at least be a unwieldy one—like a big box store where things are scattered about and you have to learn the layout as you go.

Shopping at Walmart (with Žižek)

Consumerism is something that American literature regularly takes up, if often in ambient or background ways. Here's a scene from Don DeLillo's *White Noise*, another frequent later text in my course:

> The bins were arranged diagonally and backed by mirrors that people accidentally punched when reaching for fruit in the upper rows. A voice on the loudspeaker said: "Kleenex Softique, your truck's blocking the entrance." Apples and lemons tumbled in twos and threes on the floor when someone took a fruit from certain places in the stacked array. There were six kinds of apples, there were exotic melons in several pastels. Everything seemed to be in season, sprayed, burnished, bright. People tore flimsy bags off racks and tried to figure out which end opened. (36)

This vignette is a swirl of schmaltz and unrestrained violence: punching mirrors, tearing flimsy bags, blocked entrances tarnish the burnished, bright objects, everything in season. DeLillo's high strung tensions run throughout this novel, and they are recognizable and reflective of so much day-to-day life in advanced consumer culture. Passages like this can be pulled out of *White Noise* and used for a prompt for students: here, take this to a nearby store and rewrite it using the details you find. It's both highly localizable and delightfully (maybe shockingly) generic.

I worked at a little grocery store during my last year in college, and so I have a special place in my heart for when literature inhabits these spaces—but you don't need to have worked at a store to appreciate their oddities.

One time, I had the pleasure of going to Walmart with the philosopher and cultural theorist Slavoj Žižek. It happened in 2009, when Žižek was in New Orleans to give a public talk at Loyola. Before his talk, I was scheduled to go to dinner with Žižek and two of my colleagues, John Clark and Josefa Salmón. One of them asked me if I could drive the group to dinner, and of course I said yes even though I don't really like to drive, or even be in cars for that matter. But I wasn't going to turn down this opportunity. Driving Žižek around New Orleans! I picked up Josefa, then John and Slavoj, and we headed to one of our wonderful restaurants on Magazine Street, Lilette. *Travel and Leisure* had named Lilette the "sexiest dining room in new orleans"—where else would we have taken the eminent, provocative philosopher?

It was around 5:00 when I picked up Josefa, then John and Slavoj, and we had a relatively narrow window for dinner, because the talk was scheduled to begin at 7:30. Our reservation was for 6:00, but we got to the restaurant at 5:30 thinking we'd get a drink first, or just eat early—playing it safe to have plenty of time to return to campus for the talk. But when we got to Lilette it wasn't open yet—it wouldn't open until 6:00. We drove along Magazine to find another venue nearby where we could kill thirty minutes, when all of a sudden Slavoj semi-blurted out, "Can we go to a Best Buy?!" I remember looking frantically at John and Josefa in the rear-view mirror, like *"Did he just say what I think he said?"*—and I started racking my brain to conjure the nearest Best Buy store, but I couldn't think of where one was, so I asked, "What do you need to get?"

"An ee-pode!"
"What?" (all of us asked simultaneously)
"An EE-PODE!!"
"Oh, an iPod!"

Josefa just then remembered that there was a Best Buy out in Harahan, halfway to the airport—but there was no way we would have gotten back to dinner (much less the talk) in time. So at that point I suggested the Walmart fairly close by. Then John got excited, because the Walmart on Tchoupitoulas was where some of the infamous looting had taken place after Katrina, so he thought it would be the perfect place to take Slavoj pre-dinner. (Apparently Slavoj was supposed to get an iPod for his son, or a friend of his son, or something—and they were far cheaper stateside.)

Next thing I knew I was driving down Tchoupitoulas, the street that makes a sound in the car like going over a million miniature cattle guards, headed toward Walmart.

After parking, as we walked toward the store—perhaps feeling a bit of guilt or shame, or at least somewhat out of place. But then Slavoj launched into an expostulation concerning the sheer visibility of consumerism on display here at Walmart, and how the warehouse-y, cavernous-feeling Walmart was so much better than high-end places, like, for instance, Dolce & Gabbana stores in Europe that conceal consumerism behind a sheen of glamour and minimalism. We were standing on the threshold of the store, taking in Slavoj's tirade and watching him gesticulate and begin to interpretively dominate the space, when I remembered that we were on a tight schedule. So I grabbed Slavoj's arm and led the way back to the electronics department; as someone who grew up in the United States in the 1980s and 1990s, I have a built-in sort of GPS that automatically kicks on when I enter any big box store.

The iPods were behind one of those glass cases that have locks where little doors slide open for employee-only access. So first Slavoj had to peer through the glass and select which model of iPod he wanted, and then we had to flag down a blue-vested worker to open the case and dutifully hand Slavoj the slim, plastic-wrapped Apple box. We all stood in line behind a couple buying skull and bones decorated earbuds; and then it was our turn, and Slavoj paid for the iPod in cash. Our conversation had turned from cultural critique to recent Hollywood movies, as we were surrounded by DVDs marked down to $3.99. Slavoj had recently watched *Kung Fu Panda* with his son, and was taken by some aspect of it—it had something to do with Hegel, I think.

As we left Walmart the sun was setting, and the sky was that empurpled milky orange unique to the Gulf Coast. It made me think of Michael Mann's *Miami Vice*, and my saying so ignited another spontaneous film critique from Slavoj. The dinner at Lilette was good. And so was the talk, in which Slavoj discussed the uses and misuses of violence for political ends. But the highlight of the night was shopping at Walmart (with Žižek). There was something strangely clarifying about this experience. It had to do with the place where theory and practice merge, and how everyday life is both a site for interpretation and something to live with, and through.

Teaching with film

I never received any formal training in film studies, though I picked up some tricks along the way. Film is another thing that gets lumped into the work of literature, for better or worse. It becomes another "text" to read, another cultural object to study. I refer to film stills in my writing from time to time, and occasionally I'll weave a film into a course I'm teaching. But I'll admit that teaching with film makes me uncomfortable, as it seems like a shortcut around discussion or even an injustice to the classroom, sometimes. Film also makes me anxious because it's a different kind of text, and I'm not entirely confident teaching with it, even though I am more comfortable writing about it.

One time I saw it work extraordinarily well was when I visited my friend John Garrison when he was teaching at Carroll University, outside of Milwaukee, Wisconsin. John had brought me to his campus to give a talk about airports, and he also integrated me into his classes that day. The first class was a film studies class, and they were watching Alejandro Iñárritu's 2014 film *Birdman*. I had watched the film a few days before my visit, and had reread Raymond Carver's story "What We Talk about When We Talk about Love," around which the plot wraps itself as the film unfolds.

In John's class, we watched about fifteen minutes of the film, including a part that explicitly enacts the Carver story. Then John invited the students into a spirited discussion not just about the formal aspects of the film (plenty to talk about there) or not just about how the film referred to the short story, but about all these things—including the constantly lingering enigma of what we actually talk about when we talk about love. It was a free-ranging discussion that engaged the students and in which they seemed to delight, and it occurred to me how helpful it was to have the visual examples fresh in our mind—and available on screen—even as we jumped from film to story to personal experience, and then into the more conceptual lessons that they had been studying in the course, like how metonymy works. There was something illuminating about this class, and the way John encouraged the students to draw connections across what they had read, watched, and studied for the class—as well as their own life experiences.

After lunch I took part in John's next class, a first-year writing seminar—the equivalent of an English 101. In this class they had been watching the Netflix show *Stranger Things*, and they were watching then discussing the final episode of the season. I hadn't seen any of this show, and I had only a (very) vague sense of what it was about. We watched, and then John set the students up with an ingenious challenge: I, the outsider, could ask the students anything about the episode that would help me make sense of it (and the entire show)—but they had to answer my questions either dialectically *or* in a way that referred directly to a specific scene, character, or thing in the episode we'd watched. The students buzzed with excitement as I prepared my first question. (I was flying by the seat of my pants.) We spent the next half hour going back and forth, and all the students were involved in helping me understand *Stranger Things*. Once again, it was an enchanting example of how having the visual text close to hand allowed us all to create knowledge together.

These classes were invigorating for their improvisational atmosphere as much as for their real-time learning: the students were putting their observational skills as well as their vocabularies to work, into use.

The previous semester, I had been teaching my critical theory course at Loyola, and on a whim I had decided to incorporate Jim Henson's film *Labyrinth* into the course. David Bowie had just died before the semester commenced, and he was on my mind, as well as the minds of several of my students. *Labyrinth* is arguably not the apex of Bowie's artistic career, but I've always had a soft spot for it—partly because it remains one my son Julien's favorite movies. In this class, which starts with Nietzsche, Marx, and Freud and ends with more contemporary thinkers, I started off by showing *Labyrinth* in five-minute increments at the beginning of each class, and we'd use the brief scenes as starting points to understand our daily readings. What seemed like a gimmick at first produced surprising results. My students made amusing connections: Jennifer Connelly's Sarah was an embodiment of how Marx defines alienated labor; Bowie's Jareth could be explained by way of Freud's unconscious; Hoggle utters a statement akin to Nietzsche's delineation of truth and fiction in an extra-moral sense. It was really working!

I don't know why I gave up on this approach, somewhere midway through the semester. The class became more serious, as the 2016 primaries loomed in the near distance. I wish I had kept us watching *Labyrinth*, and using the film to animate our readings. Looking back, it might even have explained some things about the absurdity of certain power consolidations—and also the power of resistance. But, somehow, I lost my nerve and reverted to standard, student-led discussions. Perhaps I was insecure about my grounding (or lack thereof) in film studies; or maybe I was getting worried that my students were getting tired of my relentless allusions to Bowie in general, and *Labyrinth* more specifically. It was also the semester before my sabbatical, and I was admittedly distracted by the promise of uninterrupted time to write, just on the horizon (as well as being preoccupied with all the logistical matters that come along with the promise of this time).

But after my trip to Carroll University the following spring, John Garrison's classes inspired me to stick with film, next time. There was another thing about John's classes: there was an almost glaring absence of interruptions or distractions by smartphones, in class. The students were really present. I'm not one to get nostalgic about the time before smartphones; I'm as plugged in as anyone, and I use the technology and its media forms with keen interest. I'm fairly liberal-minded about the presence of smartphones in the classroom as well: I don't get into policing my students' use of these things, because I accept them as a natural feature of contemporary life as we've devised it, for better and for worse. Sometimes I even call on my students to look things up on their phones, on the spot. But lately, the incessant buzzing of inbound texts and other notifications had been getting on my nerves—and my students didn't seem adept at shutting their phones off or leaving them in their bags or pockets, during class. I asked John later about this, about how he had created an atmosphere in the classroom where the students weren't constantly on their phones. He said it was nothing he did; they would *never* be on their phones in class. John conjectured that it was something about the Midwest social ethic, and a sense that the students felt responsible for their educations. I think John was being modest; I think a lot of it had to do with the alchemic vibe that he fomented in his classrooms. Whatever it was, it got me thinking about how these things are colonizing the classrooms, and how quaint the film screen had become—how, even watching and then analyzing movie scenes felt like a throwback, almost like slow reading.

Dropped my iPhone down below

There's a scene in Don DeLillo's story "Midnight in Dostoevsky" that reflects on the current omnipresence of digital media and the relative oasis that the college classroom can be. Here we are in a laughably self-serious logic seminar, where the wizardly professor Ilgauskas utters one-line axioms before the small group of anxious if intrigued students:

> "The atomic fact," he said.
> Then he elaborated for ten minutes while we listened, glanced, made notes, riffled the textbook to find refuge in print, some semblance of meaning that might be roughly equivalent to what he was saying. There were no laptops or handheld devices in class. Ilgauskas didn't exclude them; we did, sort of, unspokenly. Some of us could barely complete a thought without touch pads or scroll buttons, but we understood that high-speed data systems did not belong here. They were an assault on the environment, which was defined by length, width, and depth, with time drawn out, computed in heartbeats. We sat and listened or sat and waited. We wrote with pens or pencils. Our notebooks had pages made of flexible sheets of paper. (123)

Again, I don't want to wax nostalgic for an earlier era where college students dutifully shunned digital technology or didn't have it to begin with. I do want, as my university often encourages me to, to meet my students "where they are." But sometimes the imperative to digital mediation overwhelms me, makes me wonder about the threshold of these different ways of being: analog and digital. But of course it's never that simple, never a clear-cut binary.

Here's a story that may sound apocryphal, but this really happened. One spring day on my campus, I saw a student staring into his smartphone walk straight into a light pole. He crashed into it, stumbled backward, and looked around to see who had seen him (I was some distance away; he didn't notice me). Then he adjusted his course and went back to whatever he had been doing on his phone, unfazed.

This is one of the often ignored, occasionally painful, and sometimes embarrassing consequences of what Ian Bogost discussed in an article for *The Atlantic* called "Hyperemployment, or the

Exhausting Work of the Technology User." Hyperemployment is the endless work we do for unseen agencies, owners, and conglomerations while seemingly merely tapping away at our phones, communicating or otherwise being entertained.

Around that time I had been tuning into how hyperemployed people are on my campus. Just a few days before the student and the light pole, I had dropped my iPhone and the screen shattered. The phone still worked, more or less, but after the fall it lived on my desk in a Ziploc freezer bag, glass splinters crumbling away and accumulating gradually into tiny glinting dunes in the corners of the bag. So I had been re-experiencing my life without smartphone, and especially reconsidering how these things permeated my workplace, the university.

After a few weeks of being smartphone-free, from this altered vantage point I noticed just how busy everyone seemed to be, *all the time*. Whether in class, in meetings, or in the hallways—everyone was on their phones. And I don't say this from an easy standpoint of judgment, for I had grown so accustomed to being on my phone, justifying my near constant attachment to it by the fact that it was allowing me flexibility and freedom. I would draft essays and outline book chapters on my phone's notepad in the middle of the night. I emailed frantic students at all hours, reassuring them about assignments, missed classes, or exams. I carried on committee work long after meetings had let out, hashing out the fine points of strategic planning and SWOT analyses. I networked with remote colleagues on Twitter, and set energizing collaborations into motion. This all seemed worthwhile and productive—and I suppose it was, for the most part.

As I mentioned in the previous chapter, I'm conscious of my own cyborg existence, and I have always been a lenient professor when it comes to students and their technologies. I generally don't police their use in the classroom, and have only called students out a handful of times when their texting got too conspicuous or a facial expression suggested that a student was totally distracted by something on their phone. For the most part, I accept that these things have interpenetrated our lives so thoroughly that it is impractical and unrealistic to try to sanction their use in the classroom. Rather, figuring out the etiquette and subtlety of smartphone use in everyday life is one of the innumerable "soft skills" that should become learned over the course of college.

But that was before my smartphone hiatus.

During those weeks I found myself walking to work, feeling great. Why? Because I was not thumbing madly and squinting into my hand as I stumbled along, neck craned and tripping over the curb. I was swinging my arms and looking around. Between meetings on campus I was processing things people said as I strolled back to my office, rather than going immediately to my email inbox, replying to messages as I marched up stairs. I wasn't leaving my classes and getting directly on Slack to catch up with my collaborators; I was decompressing, and thinking about what my students brought up in our discussions.

I thought my smartphone was granting me freedom, but it was more like the opposite.

I saw these things everywhere on campus, and they were increasingly disgusting to me. This has been a difficult piece to write, because I am aware of how my criticism verges on hypocrisy, or almost depends on it: I appreciate what smartphones can do—are doing—on a daily basis. But seeing these things from a slight remove, they became revolting to me. I saw my students and colleagues tethered to their smartphones, and I wondered how these things were meshing with—or not—our ostensibly collective purpose of higher education: working together to make the world better, at least our human part in it. I realized how entangled with my smartphone I had become, and how different—how refreshing—it felt to be without it. I started reading (books!) for uninterrupted minutes in ways that I hadn't been able to for years, because I always felt the need to live-tweet whatever I was reading.

I talked to my students about this at one point during this time, extrapolating that *they too* probably didn't realize how supplementary they had become to their phones—to which they looked at me wide-eyed as if to say, "*Oh yes, we well realize this.*" The look they gave me was tragic, their faces creased in quiet despair. I told my students that I was writing a piece on my experience of being without my iPhone, and they viewed me with sardonic skepticism. "*Good luck with that*," they seemed to be thinking.

One student later emailed me a timely *New Yorker* piece called "The Useless Agony of Going Offline," in which Matthew J. X. Malady described the pointlessness of going off his handheld devices, cold turkey. He tried it for seventy-two hours, and concluded: "I would like to say that I reached some time-maximization epiphany . . . but I'm not sure that I used my time any 'better' than I normally would have during that span. I just used it differently, and found myself frequently bored as a result." Malady complains that he was basically less informed when off his handheld devices, and the piece ends with a sort of discursive shrug, as if to suggest that it is pointless to resist the hegemony burning away in our hands, pockets, and brains. It is a persuasive and shrewd article, and my student seemed to be daring me to prove Malady wrong.

But I'm not trying to make a wholesale pronouncement against these things. My relationship with my phone persisted during that time that the screen was shattered—it's just that I didn't see the thing for hours at a time, particularly when I was on campus.

I told my colleague Tim Welsh about the shattering of my iPhone, and he quickly dialed up dozens of bizarre, hilarious YouTube videos testing various fall heights and reporting the damage incurred by different devices put under various forms of duress. Take after slow-motion take of smartphones crashing into the pavement, dipped in miscellaneous liquids, and run over by SUVs. But these were tutorials ultimately geared toward protecting one's phone, or purchasing the most durable model out there. I was watching these videos from the other side, my phone having already been smashed. And perhaps the videos served as yet one more layer of entertainment and seamless commerce, no matter *why* they were dialed up in the first place.

The weird thing is that I probably wouldn't have done it on my own; I don't have the self-discipline to simply use the phone less (some people do, I understand). It took an accidental fall. And then, not wanting to spend a couple hundred dollars to replace it, or suffer through the ordeal of an average AT&T customer service experience, I just let the phone lie there in its bag, mostly inert, for several weeks. It was functional but *changed*, limited in a new way.

As I was checking my phone one day, sheathed in its plastic envelope, my partner Lara remarked how having it in a gallon-sized Ziploc freezer bag made the ridiculousness of these things wickedly obvious: we're all hanging around holding and staring into these awkward containers full of junk.

In his 1996 novel *Infinite Jest*, David Foster Wallace imagined an early twenty-first century technological stress point as our phone calls would become increasingly video-projected to others around the world—in short, a surge of things eerily like Skype and Facetime. Wallace went on to ponder what would follow: a feedback loop of increasingly reflexive self-awareness brought about by the constant demand of face-to-face communication by screen. Wallace conjured an elaborate cottage industry of ultra-realistic masks and background dioramas that would bloom alongside "videophonic" devices. Little did Wallace know that the problem would not be rampant self-presentation or its artifice. Our handheld devices are far more insidious for how they seduce us into tuning out while believing that we are tuned in. What Wallace got right was just *how much* power such communicative media could come to have over our whole bodies.

Only when you no longer carry around a phone all day—or have it at your bedside at night, to look at when you get up to pee, and first thing in the morning—will you realize how chained to it you've become. I realize that I'm making something of an arbitrary distinction, here. The Internet for many of us is so intertwined in our lives that it has become a ubiquitous dwelling space, the dispersed hearths of modern homes. Where one device ends and another begins is no simple matter.

The smartphone is a special kind of device, though: not because it merely gives us *more* of the Internet, but because the smartphone gets insinuated into our creaturely lives—it has thoroughly "extended our senses and our nerves," to borrow a line from Marshall McLuhan (4). McLuhan wrote those words in 1964. He was concerned that an "Age of Anxiety" was in the offing, thanks to new communications and entertainment technologies. Wallace, in the 1990s, was projecting this age's next phases. This is basically where we are now: in this age of post-truth where the truth of where my body ends and communicative technologies begin is relentlessly complicated by the very object in question. Being without my iPhone clarified for me many of McLuhan and Wallace's observations and insights about the addictive, accelerative qualities of our latest electronic media.

Not that I have any easy solution, beyond my own personal revelation. And it was a short-lived one. As of the time that I am revising this chapter for the book, I have a new iPhone sitting a mere inches from my fingers as I type these words, and I await its alerts and epiphanies.

Our imbrications with these devices are complex and intricate, to say the least. However, there is something to be said for the jolt of a fresh perspective. I understand that not everyone is caught in the vicious circle of checking their phone every few minutes. I recognize that many people have more self-discipline when it comes to these things. Not everyone is staring into a screen—at least, not yet.

Of course by the time I'm finishing this book I've got a new iPhone burning away in my pocket. I don't feel good about this and I would be glad to discard it, especially if I were forced to, again. I realize that this is a strange sentiment to articulate while not seeming able to actualize the effects of, on my own.

Loyola recently went "smoke free." Now cigarette smokers line a road adjacent to campus and puff together, newly organized if also somewhat abject. I wonder, though, if a "smartphone free" campus might be a far more radical—and perhaps ultimately healthier—move for a university these days.

Humanities at the airport

When I worked at an airport between 2001 and 2003, the airline I worked for gave out laudatory certificates to employees whenever passengers would report above-average customer service or any other effort that had been noticed and appreciated. On the one hand, these medal-emblazoned posters were cheesy and brimmed with the type of hollow praise proffered to alienated workers. On the other hand, though, these things were well intentioned and meaningful: they reminded us that we were working together, with and for other humans, on both sides of the counter (as well as above, at the corporate level). I look at a couple of these certificates now, saved from many years ago, and I wonder if the airline still recognizes such little instances of harmony in the maelstrom of contemporary commercial flight.

These days it can seem as though humanity has left the airport entirely, what with random fistfights breaking out, hapless passengers dragged off airplanes, racial epithets lobbed heatedly across seatbacks, families humiliated for the most minor domestic incursions, and so on. Our worst tendencies and habits come into full bloom during air travel. And people seem at once surprised by this, yet weirdly to *expect* it, too. We roll our eyes at the latest viral video of violence in the aisles, and then we turn the channel or swipe over to a new feed.

I've been trying for many years, and over the course of writing four books, to untangle the unique knots of negativity that airports have become known for. Somehow, it is perfectly acceptable to *hate* airports—even as they are also supposed to represent the apex of modern progress and cosmopolitan coexistence. How did we get to this contradictory place? And what, if anything, can those of us teaching in the humanities do to shed light on matters—and possibly even improve them?

On a flight not too long ago, I flipped through the pages of the Delta *Sky* in-flight magazine, and I noticed an article called "Higher Education in the Fast Lane." The piece surveyed a range of colleges and universities with expedited degree programs: "helping students get into the workforce more quickly and efficiently" (Delta *Sky*, May 2017, p. 87). One ad for Georgia Tech's School of Building Construction showed a worker in a hardhat and caution vest, architectural plans rolled up under his arm and giant cranes in background. The picture is one of professionalism and focused labor, and serves as a synecdoche for orderly society at large. But if the building in the background had happened to be an airport, then we would know that all this supposed orderliness would soon come to an end. Build a neat and tidy airport; invite pandemonium and civil breakdown.

When I tell people that I teach a college class about airports, they often assume I mean from a managerial or organizational standpoint: what makes them work, and how they can be improved. Sometimes I get perplexed looks when I explain that my course is about representations of airports, and how we communicate and *think* about airports. It's as though it never occurred to these people that airports and airplanes could have any other meaning or existence than the status they seem indelibly to have: functional (if barely at times), abject, ugly, and plainly understood.

This isn't just a shortcoming on behalf of airports. It's also about the role of thinking and imagination in our everyday lives, and about basic standards of human interaction, respect, and decency. This latter stuff makes what I'm talking about sound snobbish and stuffy, but I don't mean it that way. I mean it in the way that college instructors try, with great patience and care, to foster classroom environments of empathy, listening, and dialogue. Seminars—especially in the humanities—have the ability to teach students to bracket initial judgments, appreciate differences, and discuss complex, nuanced topics. These are precisely the things that we could use a lot more of these days, especially in airports and airliners.

But as evinced by the Delta *Sky* magazine article, we're increasingly skimping on college—and particularly the humanities. Foreign language programs get squeezed to the minimum or cut outright, because they are seen as too time-intensive for today's overworked student. History, literature, philosophy, religious studies—these disciplines become seen as superfluous, or they get whittled down to some hotly debated if barely tolerated "core curriculum." It is commonplace these days to refer to college as too expensive, and as out of touch with "the real world." But are we really so proud of this real world we've devised, as it comes through one of our proudest achievements, air travel? Automobile prices go up and up, as do housing prices, not to mention insurance, medicine, and healthcare—and people complain about the costs of higher education?

In fact, college-level humanities courses are what we need more of if we really want air travel to improve. And not just air travel: contemporary life at large needs more—not less—adult learning that is dedicated to reflection, understanding across differences, and respectful discourse. Disagreement and disparities of course play out in college classrooms, too—thus inviting tensions between "safe spaces" and free speech, between self-certainty and the awareness of one's own epistemological horizons. The thoughtful exercise of these things is exactly what is lacking in the day-to-day grind of flight. And corporate policy and lawmaking are not going to usher such proficiencies into bustling transit nodes. Only people can do that, of their own volition and out of a collective commitment to shared humanistic values. But these values must also be open and flexible, and they must operate irrespective of narrower value systems encoded in family, nationality, religion, and so forth. Not that these other values must be jettisoned, but to abet a heterogeneous mixture such as airspace involves, a relentless openness is requisite, along with excessive patience on all sides. (These things, too, can be practiced and honed in the college classroom.)

As I mentioned earlier, my home airfield outside of New Orleans is currently the site of a new terminal under construction, across the runways from the sprawling and mishmash existing airport. As I taxied by the skeletal frame rising from the work zone after my recent flight, it was already possible to sense the grandeur and sublime aura of what would become the new Louis Armstrong International. Still, it was hard to not also detect that this edifice was doomed—not yet completed, but already quickly on its way to becoming a cathedral of filth and waste, an arena for anger and madness.

So a simple plan: if we want to work toward more civil and humane modes of air travel, we should also be willing to invest—time, money, and thought—in the humanities. I've been talking here about higher education specifically, mainly because the lack of faith in humanities at the college level strikes me as a relevant analogue to the dearth of civility in airports. These are two concentrated realms—college and air travel—where what happens there cannot help but reflect and reinforce broader patterns and trends. We may wish for quicker paths to college degrees, as well as fast and cheap travel by air, with minimal hassle—but are we willing to accept the consequences, the attendant pressurized spaces and times? If not, we may want to think about the relationships between these realms, and how they are inescapably entwined.

But it occurs to me that this mandate would have to work the other way, too: humanities classrooms would have to be less like airports—or at least, less like airports are experienced to be in their current nadir.

Thinking space

Literature gives us space to think. It is quite literally *thinking space*. But it can also be a way to think *about* space, whether that space is a grocery store or a snowy slope.

There's a story by Lorrie Moore called "Childcare" (which later became part of her novel *A Gate at the Stairs*) that demonstrates how this works. The story takes place in the first decade of the twenty-first century, and is told from the first-person perspective of a college student looking for work. Based on preliminary content alone, it immediately presented itself to me as an apt story for university students, and so I've taught it from time to time in my classes.

The narrative is structured around restaurants, so that what seems at first to be straight storytelling gets curved by gastronomic curiosities. The story takes place in a small Midwestern town, but it quickly becomes a little looping network of ethnic foods, always ready to go global. One of my favorite first-year writing assignments is to get students to write short restaurant reviews after reading several "Tables for Two" columns from the *New Yorker*.

The restaurants don't have to be fancy; they can even include the campus dining hall, a fast fast-food, or a friend's dorm room. But I digress. (But, again, isn't that part of what the work of literature allows for?)

Near the beginning of Moore's story, the narrator mentions a meal called "Buddha's Delight" available at "The Peking Café"; by the end of the story, we are at a Perkins with a "Bottomless Pot of Coffee." One character owns a French restaurant that is a sort of present-absence throughout the story: it is mentioned repeatedly but never really *there*. The story is not ostensibly about food, per se (the narrator is *not* looking for work in a restaurant), and yet food keeps popping up, interrupting—or arguably *forming*—the narrative. This suggests a useful debate to have in class: what is the role of food in this story? This debate might also lead into another writing/observation assignment, wherein students try to discover narratives that are bubbling up from or lying dormant within their eating places of choice. (This would be rather like the obverse of Moore's story, which finds restaurants within a broader fictive landscape.)

This story can also be paired with an excerpt from Hemingway's *A Moveable Feast*, in part because of the shared preoccupations with eating out. There's also something to learn about environmental language in these two texts. *A Moveable Feast* begins: "Then there was the bad weather. It would come in one day when the fall was over" (3). Moore's story starts out similarly: "The cold came late that fall, and the songbirds were caught off guard." I ask my students how seasonal logic functions in each of these narratives. Is it just about setting, or does seasonal language *do* something specific to the setting? Perhaps it has something to do with what Heidegger called "worlding," in terms of how physical space is *disclosed*, both consciously opened up and necessarily delimited.

I think of such environmental language as "spacing"—because in the midst of such description, the narrator becomes *spaced out*, and we (the readers) are not exactly in the realm of thought, yet not totally external to it, either. This tangent might become a useful way to introduce Derrida's notion of "différance" as the spatialization of time and the temporization of space: to differ between things is also always to defer from one moment to another. Now we're in deep water, but I like to think that Derrida is always just a stone's throw away from the shallows, where the work of literature takes place.

Moore also plays with words in clever ways. For example, the narrator makes this observation concerning her college life: "In the corridors, students argued over Bach, Beck, Balkanization, bacterial warfare." Consider the spatial effects of this alliteration, asking the reader to think geographically, even geopolitically, across vast spaces and scales with different intensities. And then, how intertextuality sends the reader dashing across these external references. We can recall again Hemingway on Stein or Pound or Joyce in *A Moveable Feast*. I like this story because it invites literary and cultural allusions in prose to mingle with hypertextuality online. How is Moore's story aided by digital media ways of thinking and reading? What happens when we use a Google search to help us map routes, make translations, and follow obscure references in a story? What is the threshold of *searching* in literature?

Here's another short story for thinking space: Stephen O'Connor's dazzling "Ziggurat." This story involves an imaginative search through language and space, blending old mythologies with new media mysteries. Throughout this tale the labyrinth goes

> On and on and on. The central aisle of an airliner, the back seat of a car (stale popcorn crammed into cushion cracks), a coal mine, a hospital waiting room, a long tunnel in which a hot breeze blew first in one direction and then the other. So many varieties of emptiness. For centuries. Millennia.
>
> At every turn, the geometry of the world was reinvented.
>
> What is the Labyrinth but so much human junk? That's how the Minotaur saw it. Cathedrals, bus stations, diners, bowling alleys, subway tunnels, endless basement corridors—they all seemed profoundly pointless to him, not just because they were generally empty and unused but as a basic fact of their existence. He could tell that humans didn't share his opinion.

Maybe not, but literature can give people space to think, to contemplate what spaces matter and what spaces don't—and maybe what spaces should matter more. Thinking space is like the opposite of threatening to build walls. And it's also the opposite of mindless work.

Against careerism, for college

In the longest single section of David Foster Wallace's unfinished novel *The Pale King*, we follow the monologue of a onetime "wastoid" college student whose "transcript looked like collage art" (157). The climax of this meandering story arrives in two parts: first, a revelation occurs while our character is "just being an unmotivated lump" and "watching the CBS soap opera *As the World Turns*" (223). He realizes, at the commercial break when the network announces, "*You're watching* As the World Turns," that this is literally true, and it triggers a "dawning realization that all of the directionless drifting and laziness . . . was, in reality, not funny, not one bit funny, but rather frightening, in fact sad, or something else—something I could not name because it has no name" (225). His nihilism is punctured.

Shortly thereafter, our character is sitting in an advanced accounting class when "a substitute Jesuit" professor delivers an impromptu lecture about how accounting is nothing less than "a calling." Toward the end of his impassioned discourse, the instructor states, "You have wondered, perhaps, why all real accountants wear hats? They are today's cowboys. As will you be. Riding the American range. Riding herd on the unending torrent of financial data" (235). Our character leaves the class "in a strange kind of hyperaware daze, both disoriented and very clear"—and he goes on to change his ways, straightening up and becoming altogether dedicated to a life of accountancy.

Despite the obvious humor and linguistic playfulness, it is surprisingly difficult to conclude if Wallace is lampooning the main character and his newfound calling, or celebrating in earnest the singularity of purpose and clarity of vision that springs from the rote work of accounting. What is utterly clear, however, is that this character's career choice did not occur as a result of careful curricular planning or through the aid of support staff on his campus. It was spontaneous, and rather late in the game—after years of "classes where everything was fuzzy and abstract and open to interpretation and then those interpretations were open to still more interpretations" (157). Post-truth, indeed. And yet somehow this haphazard, pinball approach to college nevertheless ends in a decisive swerve toward a life of civil service.

I was reminded of this story as I served on a workgroup with faculty from across my campus and our career services staff concerning faculty-student advising. Specifically, we were tasked with formalizing how we integrate professional internships into the curricula of our various departments, programs, and disciplines. On the whole, our meetings were positive and productive, and I generally agree that academic departments ought to think carefully about how they prepare students for life beyond campus and after the college years are over.

But a troubling assumption kept popping up during a recent meeting: the belief that our students need, *from their first days in college*, to be thinking actively about their eventual careers.

Again, I wholeheartedly support the idea that college instructors should want to help our students discover meaningful work in the world, for the world. This is one of the things I love about teaching at a Jesuit institution: during our most intellectually far-flung class discussions, I can demand that we bring our lessons down to earth and the students don't flinch—they get it, that's what they're here for (sheer coincidence, by the way, w/r/t Wallace's "substitute Jesuit").

I take great pride in seeing my students off to good graduate programs and professional internships that then lead to jobs. One of the joys of mentoring students over the course of four years—a key, yet often underappreciated role of a tenure-track or tenured professor—is hearing from such students again one, two, or five years after graduation, once they have had some time to reflect on their education after having found a meaningful path in life, whether this means continued academic study or a full-time job in a field related (or totally unrelated) to their major. I probably get two or three letters like this a year, and these notes of gratitude always make me happy to be part of this process—which, let's admit it, can at times feel awkward, random, and ill-defined.

Yet I have to respectfully disagree with the fundamental notion that our students should be thinking about their careers from the day they set foot on campus. This seems entirely wrong for at least two reasons.

First, the idea that there are or will be stable careers in the blooming twenty-first century seems like questionable at best, and a pipedream at worst. We know better—don't we?—than to think that there are stable, sure trajectories that will see individuals steadily up a promotional ladder through to success and retirement in the chaotic and high-stakes marketplace of the post-digital economy. I graduated from college in 2000, and worked several very different full-time jobs before (and even as) I settled into graduate studies and, eventually, a teaching career. And I still have thoughts about what it would mean to "retool" myself, should my university suddenly tank or should I get fed up with the committee work and onerous demands on my life at home. (For example, I originally began writing this piece at midnight, when I should have been sleeping, but was woken up by a feeling of vague unease after the most recent meeting of that advising workgroup.) Speaking more broadly, in our frantic moment of way-past-bedtime capitalism, entire industries evaporate overnight or get subsumed by vast parent companies that themselves are no less tenuously positioned. In either case, there is no career training that can prepare one to roll with such likely transitions. The fact is if we can train our students to be one thing, it's to be *flexible*.

And this leads to the second reason I am skeptical of careerism on campus. College is precisely the place where students should not be weighed down with job-forecasting despair for a few years of their lives. Of course, we should help our seniors and/or graduate students transition into their next stages of life, but those first three years of undergraduate education should be protected for learning, for questioning, for reflection. Higher education is not vocational training, but something almost ruthlessly opposed to it. College, at least the liberal arts model of it, is about pausing to reflect on how we got to where we are now, and contemplating where we might want to go from here. And if that's not putting it audaciously enough, try this: it is about taking the space and time to think the unthinkable. And paradoxically, this might result in more flexible, better equipped individuals when it comes to actually getting into the hard work of living—earning an income, making a home (conceived broadly), paying taxes, being a good citizen, and so on.

So I cannot support the idea that our freshmen should immediately be confronted with interactive databases of career options, or be asked to delineate as-if paths to postgraduation success. This is disingenuous, blind to our historical moment, and is at odds with the rich traditions and broadening functions of higher education. I *like* seeing my students land great jobs after graduation, and I like helping them do so. I write many letters of recommendation each year, and dutifully fill out cryptically formatted reference forms. I help students craft cover letters and non-academic résumés. I take this work seriously.

But I am against the careerism that seems to be increasingly insinuating itself into college life. A student's experience should be about exploring the hitherto unknown: it should be about letting ideas and theories play in the mind and in the lab; it should be about redefining oneself, continuously—not with a clear end goal, but alert to history, sensitive to the present, and attentive to the future.

David Foster Wallace's character from *The Pale King* may in fact be an elaborate caricature, a mere drawn-out send-up of a late-twentieth-century wastoid struck by an epiphany that sends him into an as-if meaningful career. What is interesting, though, is the double-jointed placement of his character's change: it arrives first in the indolent zone of the dorm room; and second in the lecture hall, upon the words of an ardent instructor. Even if we accept Wallace's ironic tone, it is worth rallying around these parts of the college experience that cannot be plotted along the lines of any career placement rubric. The time to pause and reflect and the effects of an inspiring professor: these things when combined can result in a potent alchemy indeed.

"Alchemy" makes it sound cryptic and difficult to pin down. And it is! College is something that *should* slip through the fingers of assessment directors and helicopter parents. I haven't done the sociological research to prove this in any way, but my strong hunch—based on fifteen years of teaching and innumerable anecdotes along the way—is that truly well-rounded higher education, as opposed to the careerist model, better equips students for life beyond college. But this means supporting disciplines without easily identifiable career paths. It means letting students wander and stumble into things. It ultimately means taking college seriously, not for what it delivers but for what it is in the process: a time that flies in the face of corporatization. As much as current models try to make it otherwise, students make terrible "customers," and professors are neither mid-level managers nor highly efficient supervisors. And this is a *good* thing.

To say that higher education provides an incalculable experience is not just to employ a poetic metaphor. It's to state the truth, which is that what happens in college will never fit easily into a clearly laid-out template showing an easy path from first year to a career track postgraduation. This does not mean that colleges should not help students with postgraduation plans, but that such energy could probably be focused more effectively (if also more intensely) on the final months of college rather than imagined to be necessary from orientation day onward.

Let college be college. Then, one's working life after college might be not just a career, but might also be a *life*.

Total satisfaction

In the 1971 classic film *Willy Wonka & the Chocolate Factory*, the insatiable Augustus Gloop falls into Willy Wonka's confectionary marvel, the chocolate river. As the pudgy boy struggles to dog paddle in the cocoa current, his mother screams and shouts in alarm from the shore—"He can't swim! Do something!" To which Gene Wilder's eponymous Wonka responds by staring blankly away, gazing toward the camera and saying flatly, "Help. Police. Murder."

Re-watching the film recently, I was struck by the ingenious use of irony in this scene—and throughout the entire movie. David Foster Wallace defines irony simply: when what one *hears* does not align with what one *sees* or knows to be the truth. In the scene above, Willy Wonka clearly could not care less about the fate of Augustus Gloop or his mother's hysterical cries for help; indeed, he is worried about his *chocolate* being sullied and spoiled by coming into contact with the child's body. When Wonka intones, "Help. Police. Murder," the audience sees clearly that his words do not summon *help*, do not hail the *police*, and do not describe a *murder* (at least, not one that has happened yet).

In his 1990 essay "E Unibus Pluram: Television and U.S. Fiction," Wallace notes that irony is best used in an emergency situation: it is good at shocking us out of ingrained ways of seeing, by exploiting and exacerbating the rift between things we say and things as they actually are. This is how *Willy Wonka & the Chocolate Factory* works: by using the simple pleasures of sweets to expose many of the dark sides of consumer culture such as hidden labor, hoarding, addiction, greed, paranoia, and so on. Wonka's quirky chocolatier and his entire shrouded factory of fabulations serve to send up the grimy postindustrial world beyond.

The problem with irony, Wallace says in that same essay, is that you can't rely on it for repeated use: it doesn't offer a way to rebuild the relationship between reality and how we communicate about it. It's just really effective at revealing contradictions that are often hiding in plain sight. Irony can work very well within the constraints of a film because it sets up a dynamic of contradictory sights and sounds, or events seen and events heard, and thereby level social critique, slapstick comedy, or political commentary. What irony can't do so well, Wallace worries, is offer a constant attitude that one carries out of the movie theater and into the world—particularly when the world itself operates like Wonka's chocolate factory: promising miracles, but always with a hitch.

We see this dilemma play out more than we would probably like to admit. Just look at the next pile of junk mail that lands with a slap or thud on your table or floor. Contemporary consumer culture assures us that all our needs can be taken care of by a simple phone call, using a conveniently supplied unique code number: the perfect mattress at a once-in-a-lifetime deal. A limited time offer for two pizzas for the price of one. Refinance your home—but act fast, for this rate won't last. Personalized mass mailings with faux signatures so carefully faked that they make you look twice.

But junk mail so often gets folded directly (rightly) into the recycle bin, having barely been glanced at. We can recognize this shill without having to give it even a moment's thought. We process these incongruous glittery leaflets with utter efficiency. We know that the more earnest it looks, the more likely it is a scam. This is our landscape of everyday irony, and we are generally unfazed by it. Two recent experiences in the world of customer service drove this realization home for me.

A few weeks after setting up AT&T broadband service in our house, I received a notification of our first bill, along with a friendly reminder that I could easily access and pay my bill conveniently from my iPhone. I downloaded the "My AT&T" app onto my phone, and attempted to set up my account. Upon entering my account number and personal information, I ran into an error message that cryptically instructed me to call a certain number if I lived in Connecticut (it said nothing about Louisiana residents). Simply wanting to pay my bill and get on with life, I went to the AT&T website and looked for the option to "chat with an agent," usually the quickest way to get to the bottom of most of our modern travails.

What I encountered in this chat session was a travesty of false promises, hollow assertions of care for my individual being, and basically bumbling incompetence masked as concern. The strong, confident claims "I will help you!" and "We will resolve this together!" turned out to crumple and evaporate with the greatest of ease. They were ironic: they said one thing when I saw the reality in front of me, namely that the chat window was an indifferent medium. They did not care. (I'm not even getting into the ambiguous technologization of subjectivity here, the real dark underbelly of mass-produced assistance as it exists in call centers and behind chat programs—whether or not the "I" is a human, or a computer program.) The chat room revealed itself to be a veritable cabinet of curiosity for the many shades of irony that masquerade as sincerity, assistance, and help in our age of post-truth.

I was shuffled from "Ron G." to a second representative "Norman," neither of whom had any idea how to fix the problem. After ninety minutes of basically rehearsing the same information and describing the problem (really a silly, minor problem) again and again, I had to end the chat in order to pick up Julien from preschool.

And as Julien and I bicycled home from his preschool, I decided to simply give up; I didn't really need to pay my bill from my phone, after all. I had just thought it'd be easy. To let off the steam, however, I made a snide quip about AT&T on Twitter. Unexpectedly, this escalated me to the next level of ironies: a demand from AT&T's Twitter feed for a Direct Message so they could fix the problem. This turned into yet another customer service agent realizing they could in fact *not* help me—but *another* person might be able to—and the first customer service agent then demanded my phone number (which should have been, one would think, already associated with my account?). I explained that it was OK, I was simply going to give up—but then the DM conversation took an almost discomfiting tone: "I need to talk to you." I begrudgingly punched in my phone number, told them to try me the next morning, and closed the DM portal.

An hour later, I received a phone call from an 800-number, and I wearily (stupidly) picked up the phone. In the background I could immediately hear the anxious echo chamber of a hundred—a thousand?—other customer service agents: all haggling, troubleshooting, assuring, placating, succeeding, failing, typing, trying again. I wasn't in the mood to rehash the situation, and certainly not ready to berate this unfortunate call-center soul, and though the agent pleaded to let them help me, I said that I needed to read to my child now but they could try in the morning. The next morning, AT&T called again—but this time, "No Caller ID." A new agent with what sounded like more authority—no background noise—asked me to explain the whole situation, which I described but prefaced by saying it was all very silly and I was really just incredibly astounded by the abundance of assurances of help which never materialized. I requested a modest credit to my account, for the waste of my time—which the agent then, unsurprisingly, said they could not provide under the circumstance. I thanked the agent (for what?) and hung up the phone, annoyed but determined to just move on. Which I did. That was the end of it.

But as these things never really go away as long as we are tethered to them, and as if to reanimate this galling experience, a week later I received an email inviting me to watch a video of my bill. An accompanying visual aid in the email showed a couple enraptured by a spectacle on their computer—presumably, they were being entertained while looking at their bill. *Watch a video of my bill!* I could not help but feel as though the whole order of things was brimming on the edge of an absurd crisis, akin to what the writer Lydia Davis once described as a "strange impulse" when everything ordinary might erupt in a "moment of madness," only to snap back in place as if nothing had ever happened (186).

That same week, I had to take our car to the Subaru service center to get it looked at. Rainwater had been dripping in somewhere behind the glove box, and it was getting worse with each winter storm. The car was developing a funky smell to the point that Julien would say "Eeewww!" every time he climbed into his car seat. They couldn't locate the leak on first inspection, and so I had to leave the car over the weekend. I was told that the diagnostic fee would be $110, after which I could decide to move forward with a repair including that fee, or just pay the $110 and take the car elsewhere.

They called a couple days later, still uncertain about where the water was coming in; they had the whole front of the car taken apart. They assured me they would press on. I braced for an exorbitant cost, and Lara and I began hatching backup plans: we could sell the car; we don't really use it that often. But what about midnight emergencies? Hurricane evacuations? Our summer trips to visit family in Michigan? The situation quickly became stressful.

The next day, Trey from Subaru called. They'd figured it out: it was a clog of leaves and sticks that had accumulated over time and which had turned into a blockade of mulch in one of our air conditioner intakes; the rainwater would soak into it gradually, and suddenly spill over into the car. All cleaned out and put back together, the car was ready to pick up. I didn't ask about what this whole ordeal was going to cost me.

At the shop, I tried to act naturally. I listened as Trey described the problem; he handed me a small plastic baggy of the sodden mulch they'd extracted, and he gave me an enlarged color photograph showing where they'd taken off the cowl and vacuumed out the intake. They also gave the car a full detail. (I hadn't seen it look so clean since we'd purchased it new, six years prior.) He handed me my keys, and said "You're all set!"

"Wait, you're not charging me?" I was stunned.

"Nope, this is a one-time complimentary service. If you receive a survey like this in the mail, we'd really like to know that we did everything we could have done for you." He waved his finger over the highest rating line of fill bubbles, the tens. "If there's anything I can do right now to make sure you are totally satisfied, just tell me."

I was dumbfounded, grateful, agog—and I grabbed my keys and practically sprinted out of there before they changed their minds.

In some ways, my experience at the Subaru garage could be seen as the exact opposite of my experience in the Kafkaesque world of AT&T customer service. However, the chilling thing is that they both operate at the exact same level of everyday irony. Trey was wonderfully generous, but did he really mean that he would do whatever it would take to make me totally satisfied? No. I couldn't, for instance, have followed up with "You know, actually, this Impreza is getting a little tight now that we have two children; could we just swap it right now for a new Forester, and call it even?" The generosity was a calculated move to generate positive survey results—which I gladly gave to Trey—but only to maintain the system that is in place, never to change it. It also, of course, is an attempt to keep me as a loyal customer. But not for the transcendent purpose of *total satisfaction*. That phrase is ironic. It's just not true; it can't be. And yet, it flourishes—and we don't even flinch. *Total satisfaction* shares the same post-truth kernel that resides at the center of "Make America Great Again," which would come to prominence a few years after this story.

Subaru prides itself on being a car company to which its customers are fiercely devoted. As its website enjoins, Subaru drivers "love every mile." Around that time, a website banner photograph displayed a father sitting on the back bumper of a Subaru with three kids, parked on a dirt road in green country. They are holding a radio-controlled airplane, and they emanate attitudes of deep contentment. But don't look too close, or you may detect some malaise lurking right under the surface.

Clearly anyone who has taken a road trip with a child (not to mention three) has had the experience of *not* loving every mile. Moreover the day-to-day grind of a commute, the frenzied weekly grocery haul, the airport run—all these ordinary drives regularly fail to inspire our deepest feelings of affection along the way. It sounds very nice, and Subarus may indeed be great cars—but this has nothing directly to do with *love*. It has to do with precise engineering, high-quality manufacturing, and a savvy marketing model. Love is ironic: it is what you *hear* from Subaru, but not what you *see*. What you see is a car that works pretty well, most of the time. Subaru's hook is a brazen extension of the postmodern, self-aware smarmy commercials of car companies in the 1990s that Wallace describes in "E Unibus Pluram." For Subaru is using irony in the earnest guise of sincerity.

The critic Raymond Williams once lamented "real advertising" as "an ordinary form of public notice," as opposed to "pseudo-advertising" which breeds "a stimulation of consumption" and "the continuance of . . . crazy peddling" (87). In my encounters with both AT&T and Subaru, I met the contemporary specter of Williams's fear, a bold new irony that, as Wallace anticipated, becomes tyrannical in its pervasiveness: there's simply no way out of it, since to feel like you're satisfied is to have been absorbed into its endlessly productive force.

Consider one final example: this one from the work of literature, proper. At the end of each semester for each course I teach, my university provides me with course evaluations that my students are to fill out and return to the dean's office. These forms are ostensibly driven at improvement, at making my teaching (and the product, *higher education*) better. They aim at total satisfaction. But the more I teach, and the more I witness my colleagues' and students' generally passive consumption of these prolific evaluations, and the more I see things on college campuses basically remain the same—I have come to realize that these forms too are strictly ironic documents.

This is not to say that the intention of the administration, faculty, or students is callously or even consciously ironic as we all dutifully distribute, fill out, and collect and tabulate the results of these evaluations. Rather it's that no one, not even the most entrenched director of assessment or the most earnest student, really expects anything to change—at least not immediately, not for them. The more that our course evaluations seem to be geared toward improving the individual experience of the student or the performance of the individual instructor, the more they assure a sort of diffusion of responsibility and a general resignation toward things as they are. It is precisely the acting out of this evaluative, personalized ritual, semester after semester, that ensures that things keep going more or less as is, and that no one ever seriously evaluates or reflects on the whole mess. The purpose of the evaluation is not to evaluate but to have conducted evaluation.

And yet, perhaps paradoxically, the mess of higher education is OK! This is what the liberal arts excel at, in fact: exposing students to a wide range of ideas, disciplines, approaches, and they quite intentionally do not fit together neatly or evenly. Dots get connected spontaneously, in sudden, mind-blowing epiphanies; and some curricular dots remain in isolation, forever, but nevertheless part of what makes one a "well-rounded" individual. One might go as far as to say that the truth of college (and life) is messy; it is to adopt a *post-truth* stance to think that higher education (or life!) can be made clear-cut, easy to evaluate on a simple form and improve accordingly.

On a smaller scale, what I love about teaching college is that what happens in the classroom is totally, inescapably singular: you can never step into the same college course twice. The notion that higher education is (or should be) standardized or concretely measurable is patently false, because college is a relatively loose structure that facilitates (but necessarily flexibly, messily) an experience of dynamic personal change. It is not a coincidence that this experience often aligns with the dynamic, transformative years when people shift—however awkwardly or gracefully—from child to adult. One's whole experience in the world—*of* the world—changes.

This is what happens in college classes, at least at their best: people are given the time and space to develop, which means to change their minds, which means to go through a process that is mysterious, quasi-spiritual, and (hopefully) somewhat revelatory. Whether we are talking about biology, painting, or philosophy—I'm sorry, the experience of education at the college level can't be measured so as to be "improved" for the individual student/consumer. It's rather a one-time deal for each student (barring, perhaps, things like transferring to a new school or returning to school later in life). To cast higher education in terms of measurable deliverables, assessable skills, immediate payoff—is to say something ironic about it. It's impossible to evaluate the mess that is true education, and yet we keep doing it, and assuring our students and ourselves that it's for good reason, that it will result in something better.

In truth, all such promises of direct improvement, total satisfaction, and final resolution are false. They are like Willy Wonka's perfectly curated fantasyland that offers an infinity of treats, with no stomachache to follow. Of course, the golden ticket holders in the chocolate factory do learn hard lessons, over time; and by the end of the film, irony gives way to sincerity, and a gift.

In his famously enigmatic essay from 1936, "The Work of Art in the Age of Mechanical Reproduction," the cultural critic Walter Benjamin observed that as methods of mass production made their way into modern society, "the sight of immediate reality has become an orchid in the land of technology" (233). Benjamin was interested in how art could be revolutionary, even as it takes on new aspects and forms that stem from technical reproducibility and which threaten art's age-old "aura." Benjamin wasn't trying to save "immediate reality" from mass production, though; he was just noting that it becomes more rarified. But little did Benjamin know that the orchid itself could turn out to be made of candy: redolent, scrumptious—and fake. We have reached a point where the whole world of everyday consumer life is candy colored and hollow—a new irony everywhere we look. Promises and appeasements are overflowing from the mouths of whispering call agents and presidents alike. And nothing is what it says it is. Help. Police. Murder.

In defense of small things

On such a groundless landscape, where does one find firm footing? Things like the News app on an iPhone can make the world seem dizzyingly large and fast and yet also in one's palm, begging for a tap or a swipe. One small thing I've done in this age of post-truth is to delete the News app from my phone. I don't need to see breaking news items that much, that often. If I still love the basic mission of liberal arts education, it is for how it stands against the viral, compulsive logic of things like the News app in which information and stories are controlled and curated for one's *total satisfaction*. The News app may look like a mere small thing, but its effects are no small matter.

Far more bulbous, a liberal arts education is usually conceived of in terms of a clustering of classes across a range of fields and disciplines. Such an approach results, so the story goes, in the "well rounded" individual who has an appreciation for the sciences and the humanities, who can work with raw data and with subtle hermeneutics, at turns, and who understands history as well as the complexities and nuances of the contemporary moment. This understanding is relatively accurate as a zoomed-out view of how the liberal arts work. But then there are other parts of a liberal arts education. Smaller parts—but still bigger than the apps on our smartphones.

There are of course those weightier things, such as David Foster Wallace talked about in his Kenyon commencement speech "This is Water": learning to recognize the difference between cultivating awareness and sensitivity, and sliding into the mindless mode of the "rat race." But I'm not talking about this sort of heaviness, not exactly.

When I think back on my own liberal arts education at Hillsdale, I realize that there were many small things that contributed to my overall experience—things that weren't necessarily planned in advance or that would show up on my transcript but were absolutely meaningful for me.

For instance, I recall when my English professor drove me up to Ann Arbor to hear Gary Snyder read from a new collection that had just been published. Our little college was about forty-five minutes south of the University of Michigan, and we were far less likely to get a speaker like Snyder on our campus. Another English professor—an early modernist who took sympathy on me for my lack of curricular planning—agreed to do an independent study on Shakespeare and nature so that I could satisfy a certain graduation requirement. Then there was the time when a favorite philosophy professor went along with a gaggle of us students to see the film *The Matrix* when it first hit the theaters. We saw the movie and then went to a pub to discuss the film in relation to various readings and class discussions we'd had. In the spring when the weather turned nice, my Latin professor would take us outside with a big bucket of colorful chalk and we'd do our translations on sidewalks around the quad, in garish pinks, yellows, and blues. This might just seem whimsical or puerile, but it made some pedagogical sense: changing the context of learning to make the lessons stick.

There were doubtless many other small things that shaped my education, too—but I'm focusing here on the ones that involved my professors. As a professor now, I often find myself thinking about all the parts of the job that go unremunerated, but that are also immeasurably *part of the job*. This might be a last-minute, unplanned "office hour" with a student that ends up being a walk through the park, on my way home. Or it might be the senior thesis, which is a voluntary overload credit, in terms of a teaching assignment, but which ends up (usually, hopefully) as a student's capstone experience reflecting in unpredictable ways the sum total of their education, thus far. Or it can simply be a coffee or a beer bought for a student over an impromptu session of life-advice-giving or calming near graduation trepidations.

These small things add up, in at least two ways: they are the uncompensated, incalculable parts of the job; but they are also the things that can result in lifelong memories for students. They are parts of the job that can make the whole enterprise seem worth it: when you actually help someone make a good decision, or at least maybe avoid a bad one.

A few years ago, my own university went through a prolonged and at times confusing "financial equilibrium" process, dovetailing with a general assessment phase. It all amounted to nothing. After a turnover of administration and consulting firms, we're now involved in a new organizational model aimed at a "bankable plan." Newly formed "work streams" meet regularly and occasionally announce major initiatives and future projections—but with minimal details, and descriptions of actual changes "sanitized for confidentiality requirements." In all this high-level analysis the ordinary parts of day-to-day college life go unappreciated, often dismissed as purely anecdotal.

All this can lead to cynicism. The less grandiose parts of a college education seem more important than ever, to me: learning the basics of adult communication, professionalism, punctuality, responsibility—maybe even knowledge of a discipline. And then there are all the even smaller things, those things that make the job meaningful—especially when there are salary freezes or threats of "across the board" cuts. In a time when administrators are swayed only by data crunches and comparisons with peer institutions and "best practices," the slow, small-scale impact of each single class, each one-on-one interaction with a student—these things go unnoticed.

It is an economic paradox, of sorts, that the parts of this job that are about uncompensated *giving* are also those parts that *give back*—and that these things might also be the very measures by which we defend this model of education. If we are really interested in educating "the whole person," then we professors have to be whole people, too—with all the uncertainties and failed points of satisfaction that come with that excessive definition.

Being a professor is still a great job, for so many reasons. And a lot of those reasons will always necessarily remain unquantifiable. This doesn't mean professors shouldn't work hard to be fairly compensated, or find ways to recognize and be rewarded for the small things—but just that we should also acknowledge that there are many things we do on our campuses (and off) for our students that will always fall through the cracks of assessment and reimbursement, but will nevertheless benefit our students in inestimable ways. It's the small things that count.

Environmental studies, with no limits

One time I was chatting with a colleague in the hall and I mentioned that I'd just come from our monthly Environmental Studies meeting on campus. My colleague, apparently unaware that I was affiliated with Loyola's Environmental Studies program, looked at me quizzically and asked, "Oh, do you get out much?" Apparently I didn't strike my colleague as the outdoorsy type.

I didn't really know what to say. At first I sort of stammered, "You mean, like personally do I get out much? Um, not really, these days . . ."—feeling guilty about my lack of serious outdoor activity of late. Then I caught myself and I said, "Well yes, actually, I take Julien on a walk to the river nearly every morning." But I think my hesitation ruined my chance at proving my outdoorsiness: I had come across as uncertain about what the question even meant in the first place.

The truth is that I *am* uncertain about the "out" in my colleague's question. Sure, I am drawn to the ecotone between the river and the levy, where packs of feral cats cruise and redwing blackbirds alight in the *salix* groves. But I'm just as enchanted by the smashed green glass of Heineken bottles, piles of red crawfish carcasses discarded during parties the night before, crumpled Cool Ranch Doritos bags, and the oversize chicken-wire retainers holding back the bulging boulders of the riprap. This is the great outdoors, and it's big enough to contain everything. In fact, it doesn't even contain—it just keeps spreading outward.

But then again, I do know what my colleague meant. I've spent time in the mountains and on the rivers. I am easily perturbed and annoyed by the cultural inanities of manicured lawns, pretentious fences, terrible drivers in oversize vehicles, and the hyperreal generic playgrounds distributed throughout cities and suburbs alike. The latter, these playgrounds, are particularly galling settings: places that would hardly seem to count as *environmental*. That's why I prefer to go to the river, after all. And yet, here is where some forays into the field of *object-oriented ontology* intervene in an instructive (if also complicating) manner. Linger with me at the playground, a perhaps unexpected place for the work of literature in an age of post-truth.

Around New Orleans, I've noticed a recurring playground figure. It's a broad plastic wavy board about a foot above ground, usually bolted to the legs of a climbing structure, attached to the board is a steering wheel and an inset speedometer, and next to this is a six-speed shifter (with reverse).

On the reverse side of the board there is the visage of a car's front and bumper, and where the license plate should be, a message appears: No Limits.

At this particular playground on St. Charles Avenue, the No Limits car shows up in three distinct places among slides and swings strewn about the rubberized ground. Not only is it ubiquitous around town, then, but it also manages to disseminate throughout individual playgrounds.

When we are at this playground, sometimes Julien will steer the steering wheel or shift the shifter. But just as often, he'll ignore it and go for something else, either on the structure or nearby in the dirt.

What should one even call this thing? Is it a toy? An activity? A training station? A not-so-subtle form of car-culture indoctrination? Whatever it is, it seems like the antithesis of an ecological object: this is hardly an icon of environmental studies.

This thing brings to mind Roland Barthes's essay "French Toys," in which seemingly innocent playthings are explained to "*literally* prefigure the world of adult functions" (53). Far from being innocuous objects of play, for Barthes such toys severely limit a child's imagination: "faced with this world of faithful and complicated objects, the child can only identify himself as owner, as user, never as creator; he does not invent the world, he uses it: there are, prepared for him, actions without adventure, without wonder, without joy" (53–54).

Yet even before recalling Barthes's theory about toys, my initial reaction to the categorical confidence of this idea of No Limits had been strong skepticism, if not an outright *Bullshit!*

No limits? You bet there are limits, and—attachment parenting notwithstanding—that's what child rearing is all about, right? Setting limits, enforcing them, redrawing lines when necessary—however you do it, it's all about *limits*. To suggest that there are "no limits" undermines the hard work of parenting, and sets up false hope in the minds of the children. Life is riddled with limits, and it's precisely these ordinary and banal limits that must be come to terms with, navigated, or otherwise encountered every day.

Then there is the matter of the No Limits imperative appearing *on a car*. Even Subaru wouldn't be so bold as to claim No Limits. And here is where my ecological intuition kicked in: to see this vaguely New Age, negatively positivist language aimed at children on the front of an oncoming, simulacral *car*—it's all rather appalling. In the context of a children's play area (the future of humankind, etc.), it seems pernicious to yoke the idea of limitlessness to the culture of automobility. We don't actually believe that cars represent the final frontier of personal mobility, do we? Or that cars themselves have *no limits* to where they can go or where they will deliver us—as much as the latest Buick or Hyundai ad might like us to think it so? No Limits is cheesy marketing at best, and critical imagination stunting at worst. Let's not even get into fossil fuel consumption, scarcity of resources, what roads do to ecosystems, and, as the sage Slavoj Žižek might put it, "so on and so on."

In other words, "No Limits" would seem definitively to be no way to conceive of *environmental studies*.

One morning, I stood in the playground thinking about the absurdity of No Limits as Julien played nearby, engaging the ridiculous dashboards and at times simply bypassing them for other intriguing things. I was entertaining my normal internal rant when I was abruptly caught off guard by a ruthless intrusion of questions and uncertainties. What if I were to take this object more seriously, both as a semiotic register and as a thing in its own right?

First off: what did "no limits" mean, anyway? How seriously should I—or *could* I—take it? If it were a message to the children, could it possibly serve as a clever critique of the very object of mobility it adorned? Could it be saying, perhaps, that there is *no limit* to how the car itself could be played with, re-imagined, outmoded, recycled? Who was I to say what the "no limits" referred to, anyway? Strictly speaking, maybe there *are* "no limits" when it comes to existence—what do I know? Wouldn't Hegel say that the dialectical quality of the world is precisely what escapes all the limits of finitude? Is it so bad that my boy might be having a sincere if low-grade encounter with Hegelian *Geist* while playing at the park?

And even if I didn't want to open up those particular philosophical floodgates, weren't there still yet other ways that "no limits" could be more creatively conceived? Perhaps in a depthless-experience kind of way—for who can possibly fathom the fractal quality of each car's ability to absorb all the traces of conversations had, music played, French fries pressed into seat cushions, geographical expanses covered, bug splats endured, thefts of car stereo or car entire—in short, each car's long and various life span? Indeed, isn't this precisely what Thomas Pynchon's character Mucho Maas, in *The Crying of Lot 49*, thinks about the used cars he sells—a thought process that send him into an existential tailspin? (For I had been teaching the novel that week, and the passage was fresh on my mind.) How did Mucho describe those cars, a description seemingly without limits? People bring in their used cars to the sales lots,

motorized, metal extensions of themselves, of their families and what their whole lives must be like, out there so naked for anybody, a stranger like himself, to look at, frame cockeyed, rusty underneath, fender repainted in a shade just off enough to depress the value, if not Mucho himself, inside smelling hopelessly of children, supermarket booze, two, sometimes three generations of cigarette smokers, or only of dust—and when the cars were swept out you had to look at the actual residue of these lives, and there was no way of telling what things had been truly refused (when so little he supposed came by that out of fear most of it had to be taken and kept) and what had simply (perhaps tragically) been lost: clipped coupons promising savings of 5 or 10¢, trading stamps, pink flyers advertising specials at the markets, butts, tooth-shy combs, help-wanted ads, Yellow Pages torn from the phone book, rags of old underwear or dresses that already were period costumes, for wiping your own breath off the inside windshield with so you could see whatever it was, a movie, a woman or car you coveted, a cop who might pull you over just for drill, all the bits and pieces coated uniformly, like a salad of despair, in a gray dressing of ash, condensed exhaust, dust, body wastes—it made him sick to look, but he had to look. (4)

Who was I to foreclose the possibilities of cars? Why not consider "No Limits" in all its vastness and reality? In fact, by getting caught up in my internal debate, hadn't I already invited a kind of limitless speculation to occur, as in Mucho Maas's own rambling meditation on used cars?

There I was, puzzling over the implications of the No Limits cars, pacing around the play structures and muttering to myself. Meanwhile, Julien was trying intently to wedge woodchips into the craggy bark of a giant live oak that rose above the playground—he was talking to the chunks of mulch, coaxing them into the grooves of the tree and softly saying "oh, no!" whenever they fell to the ground.

Suddenly I recalled one of my favorite Nietzsche aphorisms, about how human maturity "consists in having found again the seriousness one had as a child, at play" (83). Julien and I were two sides of the same coin—varieties of seriousness, two practitioners of playground philosophy.

That would be a tidy way to end the essay—but it's not the end of the story. For there is a third side of this coin to consider, and it is a deceptively capacious side: it's the circular *edge* where all the other stuff exists.

Julien and I weren't alone in this scene, thinking about No Limits or playing with bark. There was the tree, too—as well as the toy car with its six-speed shifter and steering wheel. The way the nut and bolt connected the steering wheel to the plastic panel, and how the wheel wobbled on certain No Limits panels that have loose bolts. The shade from the tree. Ants coursing around in lines or scouting solo, on their own. Our stroller, parked at the edge of the playground. A weed-whacker-ravaged Capri-Sun silver drink sack, sitting abandoned in the grass. Nano-particles wafting over from across the street, where a leaf blower was doing its work. A Land Rover driving by, bass thumping. Cicadas droning in the upper canopy of the live oak. Spanish moss hanging down. A helicopter chopping above. Cumulonimbus clouds building a few thousand feet above that. Mushrooms decomposing leaves, back on the ground. In short, the realm of "serious play" was all around, and it was about way more than just us humans. Maybe it's not we humans who are or become "mature"—maybe it's the *world*, in all its various forms, at all scales.

This is where traditional frameworks of environmental studies explode, because they fail to describe fully any precise scale of life. The No Limits playground feature was never just about cars and the humans who make and use (or abuse) them. It was always also about plasticity and metallurgy, about recycled rubber ground-padding, dust patinas, and rain stains on plastic. It was about how certain size woodchips could be wedged into the gear shifter, and how the splinters from the wood mix with Cheez-It cracker crumbs and nestle within the plastic nooks, making perfect bivouacs and breeding sites for Indian Meal Moths, reflexively prompting elaborate pest management services, teams of brightly colored pickup trucks laden with vats of insecticide and spraying devices driving around town.

Object-oriented ontology does not offer any easy answers to questions of ecology or environmental studies. But what it prompts is a heightened demand to pay attention to the things that are all around, incoming and constantly retreating: from the playful act that turns a tree into a living game, to an inert toy that becomes an uncanny interlocutor of sorts; from the fern clusters growing out of the live oak bark, to a thought that sinks into a deep pool of questions. It may not look like other more obvious forms of environmental action or discourse (hiking through meadows; claims like Earth First!), but object-oriented ontology nevertheless provokes a kind of intense awareness of the webs of things around, sticky and porous at once. When you take this philosophical project seriously, you become what Ian Bogost calls an "alien phenomenologist."

What do alien phenomenologists do? Their job, according to Bogost, is "to go where *everyone* has gone before, but where few have bothered to linger" (34). From this perspective, we have to rethink Nietzsche's point about maturity. The idea isn't that what adults perceive as seriousness is in fact identical to the experience of child play. Rather, the seriousness of a child at play would be closer to the mind-boggling potential of adults to *lose* their own kind of human-centered seriousness, and to be amazed by ordinary things—human and non-human, without clear distinction. It's something to strive after, but not because it results in more clarity or purpose. Human maturity, here, is about the *world's* (im)maturity, in all its expanding multitudinous forms and texture.

It's a state to rediscover, but in the way that one rediscovers the otherworldliness of a favorite children's book, elaborate and enchanting. To really allow oneself to fall into this state, or to take it seriously as something that we might consciously do more frequently—this is far more perilous, because the human realm becomes less exceptional, and less stable as a center. In this alternative state of maturity (which will often resemble immaturity), you find yourself in a realm of countless others, and falling through layers upon layers of existence (upward *and* downward). It's dizzying, but it can also be humbling and wonderful—because it's never final. For meanwhile, like a concentrating toddler, you are always on to something else, lingering anew, where objects abound.

Environmental studies, then, isn't about going somewhere in particular; rather, it is about studying the ecological shot through *anywhere*. This turns out to be another perhaps surprising part of the work of literature in an age of post-truth: it is environmental studies, with no limits.

College: It's a mess

One morning I arrived on my campus to discover a new sculpture in our Academic Quad, which already had about eight sculptures situated with plenty of breathing room around the lawn. In a year of salary freezes, budget cuts, and no newly approved tenure-track faculty lines, some of my colleagues were outraged that the university was apparently spending money on new and exorbitant appearing art. It didn't help that this particular sculpture vaguely resembled a giant pair of testicles—or in the offhand description of one of my students, it looked "like a big droopy ball sack."

A couple hours later a team of workers in cargo pants and black T-shirts began to install yet *another* sculpture in the center of the quad: this one was a precarious stack of wooden chairs that interlocked legs in an intricate pattern. What was going on here? By the afternoon we realized what was happening: it turned out they were props. It was all for a movie.

Unbeknownst to any of us (at least my colleagues and students who wandered around these new sculptures, angry or bemused), a scene from *22 Jump Street* was being filmed on our campus, and the film crew was using our sculpture garden as a typical college setting. Only it apparently wasn't typical enough—there weren't an adequate number of sculptures for it to *really* look like a college quad on the big screen. Additionally, one of these simulacral sculptures—the rumors were beginning to circulate—would be destroyed in the making of this scene. (Car chase, wreck.) In order to make a college, you've got to break some art.

The next morning when I took my literature and environment students outside for class, we noticed that all the maroon Loyola signs had been concealed, and industrial-blue signage that read Metropolitan City State College was displayed liberally throughout the quad. We were now sitting in a newly renamed Meditation Sculpture Garden (stressed by the italicized subtitle as a *Quiet Zone*). It was a surreal class that morning, discussing the *Oxford English Dictionary's* definition entry of "wilderness" while stern grips and sweaty set assistants bustled around us, clamping things down and positioning hidden clusters of spotlights, making our college campus into a more dazzlingly authentic looking place for higher learning. *Wilderness*: "1. c. A piece of ground in a large garden or park, planted with trees, and laid out in an ornamental or fantastic style, often in the form of a maze or labyrinth."

This was hitting a little too close to home, as the quad around us was at once ours and not ours, the actual Loyola University New Orleans and an imaginary Metropolitan City State College at once, a sculpture garden of real and irreal art pieces. Having recently made it successfully through the tenure application process at my university, I decided to quip on Twitter that I had been promoted to associate professor of English at Metropolitan City State College. And my friends and followers favorited, retweeted, and congratulated me—in earnest or ironically, no way to tell. Poe's Law proven once again.

A few days later in my David Foster Wallace seminar a student asked with sincerity what the point had been of slogging through a particular novella-length story. "The Suffering Channel" is a text that can seem to be little more than (and maybe too much, at that) densely layered dark satire throughout its many pages of thick description and spiraling corporatese. It is also, arguably, a drawn out poop joke. My student put me on the spot, if kindly and apologetically, admitting that her question was off topic and unfair—but I tried to embrace the spirit of her frustration. What were we doing there, anyway, when there were so many more important things in life to be spending our time on, as Wallace seems to be getting at in this story? In an age of post-truth, rambling abstract discussions can seem gratuitous at best and enabling at worst: here we are contemplating irony as the juggernauts of power and dominance chug onward *using* irony to their advantage.

I recognize this skeptical look on my students' faces more and more, and it makes me squeamish because I understand the feeling. In a fumbling way, I recalled and paraphrased my mentor Timothy Morton's line from *The Ecological Thought*, about how pausing and reflecting can be a radical act, and I went on about how taking time to engage art, and lingering on paradoxes and contradictions—these things might actually be forms of resistance in a culture that essentially wants us to hurry up and consume: favorite, like, retweet, buy now, more more more more. But even as I said this I could feel how self-justifying it was, us sitting outside in a circle on a balmy New Orleans afternoon, me pontificating about the inestimable value of college to my sweet and smart but likely (understandably) terrified students on the brink of their lives in the so-called real world (that chestnut drives me crazy).

While writing this book I've found myself at once acutely aware of the privilege and relative aloofness of the college experience, while also feeling the absolute urgency of this space, this time. I'm well aware that higher education is in something of a crisis mode as it attempts to adapt and adjust to the times, times that are themselves fleeting and perpetually obsolescing faster than most will admit. As administrations hurry to optimize hybrid and online delivery platforms, I see a willful denial of the fact these things too are destined to change again, possibly quite quickly, in the oncoming years. I see the seminar space as something truly resilient and able to weather these fast times—indeed, as a place in which to slow down and see these times for what they are (no easy task, to be sure).

But I also realize that college—and especially this more traditional model of college—is way too expensive, and that the dwindling tenure system and corollary precarious labor conditions of adjunct instructors are coming to a head, unable to sustain the very model that I am championing. I recognize the perceived gap between traditional education and the contemporary trends (flip that classroom!), and I'm not sure what to do about it: how to bridge this gap, and when to—frankly—ignore it. These things keep me up at night, and at my lowest points, these messy issues make me feel like I'm a relic of something outmoded, and that I should just quit.

Still, there is something about when it works: when the discussions get intense, when I see students making spontaneous connections across their courses, across disciplines. When they get truly excited about research projects, and their creativity and imaginations merge with new ideas and discoveries in texts, in the world. There is something that I'm adamant about preserving, even bolstering, as liberal arts education gets increasingly routinized as well as scrutinized for its outcomes and inefficiencies.

But higher education of the whole person—even admitting the problematic nature of that very idea, the "whole person"—this is not something that can really be measured or seen through data. It just can't. It's a mess, but one that I'm still glad to participate in—if not ever finally clean up, exactly.

Thinking critically about critical thinking

A couple weeks after the *22 Jump Street* incident, I listened to a Diane Rehm Show podcast called "Worries about the Future of Liberal Arts Colleges." Among some of the more insightful anecdotes and expected axioms offered throughout the program, I was struck by the absence of a certain phrase: there was no mention of *critical thinking*. This phrase has been used to the point of exhaustion to describe something inestimable about liberal arts education, and has become something of a placeholder to describe without describing what college is good for.

Critical thinking: it's a ubiquitous phrase on syllabi (especially for first-year courses), stated as a learning objective or assessable outcome—but it's something equally difficult to pin down or articulate with any exactitude. What is critical thinking? Well, maybe you know it when you see it—or when you *do* it. Or perhaps you recognize when it *isn't* happening, because you notice that everyone is acting like robots (like docile robots, anyway). Whatever it is or is supposed to be, it's a phrase that has come to give me the creeps, because when I hear it or see it, it's often in the service of something mandatory, obligatory, required—it's a rhetorical tic that becomes ritualized and normalized, and is often uttered in the context of drawn-out committee meetings to nodding faculty. In short, the phrase often comes to mean the opposite of something produced by sudden break, rupture, or flash of insight (the word "critical," my old professor Marc Blanchard used to frequently remind his students in graduate seminars, is etymologically related to "crisis").

So the point is that "critical thinking" as a phrase often gets trotted out in rote ways, as a vague aim of a certain kind of pedagogy. But if you put someone on the spot and ask what it really *is*, you will likely induce some incredible facial expressions that veer between puzzlement and horror, depending on the person, usually ending with this: "You know, it's like, thinking *critically* about things!" Needless to say, this sort of response doesn't win accolades in terms of definitional clarity or utility.

Still, it was odd to suddenly *not* hear this phrase (or at least, not as a recurring trope) on a radio program focusing on the value of liberal arts education. It was as if all the prior repetitions and insistences had set it (i.e., "critical thinking") up for all too easy dismissal. The guests on the show discussed liberal arts in terms of creating "well rounded" subjects individuals, but not one of the participants pressed the point that education might actually involve developing a critical stance toward the world. (Save Catharine Bond Hill of Vassar, who continually and admirably tried to steer the conversation back to economics.) Because that's really what critical thinking is, isn't it? It's being able to have—and hone, and articulate—a constructively contrary attitude toward things in society or culture that are in need of change, but toward which most people shrug and go about their business.

Critical thinking is a comportment toward the world as it is, with a mind to *changing* it for the better. Isn't this what we hope for out of college education, at its best? That the students will, in learning about the world from a range of disciplinary perspectives, actually want to change it for the better? Because if so, then all of the rampant and tepid talk about higher education in terms of professionalism, technological proficiency, vocation, career training, this is all a lot of very dull resignation, a stoical attitude that things are basically set in stone now, and all we can do is shape ourselves around the mold. Oh, and make sure you get some critical thinking along the way; tick that box.

One day in my David Foster Wallace seminar we were tackling the very short story "Incarnations of Burned Children." Four students in the class simultaneously and enthusiastically declared that they had read and discussed this story in their Introduction to Creative Writing course a couple years prior. I asked what they had learned about the story, and not one of them could produce anything beyond this rather vague answer: "I think it was supposed to teach us how to tell a story." I pushed them to recall the specific lessons the story might have held for beginning creative writers. Blank looks. I asked what sort of textbook this story had appeared in, and one student described the book, mentioning that it was "the kind of anthology with a list of 'critical thinking' questions after each piece." At this, my ears perked up. What sort of questions were these? No one could remember any of these questions, even in the most general terms.

I let it go, and we went on to have a lively discussion about Wallace's manipulation of time and the red herrings of symbolism throughout the story. But the spectral "critical thinking" questions stayed with me, aggravating this nagging interest I have concerning this phrase. How does this phrase function, and what do we want from it? When is it a handy if nebulous outcome, and when does it get dropped in favor of more concrete skills?

Digging into these questions, and mostly wanting to locate a firm definition, I discovered a two-tiered explanation of this phrase on the University of Louisville's website, on a page called "What Is Critical Thinking?" It reads, in part:

> After a careful review of the mountainous body of literature defining critical thinking and its elements, UofL has chosen to adopt the language of Michael Scriven and Richard Paul (2003) as a comprehensive, concise operating definition:
> Critical thinking is the intellectually disciplined process of actively and skillfully conceptualizing, applying, analyzing, synthesizing, and/or evaluating information gathered from, or generated by, observation, experience, reflection, reasoning, or communication, as a guide to belief and action.

On the one hand, this definition seems fairly airtight and straightforward: critical thinking is the application of information to shape decisions. Easy enough. On the other hand, this definition is so capacious as to nearly explain away the very thing it seeks to describe. Critical thinking is an "intellectually disciplined process"— overarching (or sidestepping) all disciplines per se. It involves a chain of "and/or" activities that can happen in so many contexts (including the most ordinary "experience") that one would be hard pressed to find a place where it *isn't* happening, on some level.

Critical thinking becomes a sort of mental Swiss army knife, able to unfold a range of analytic tools depending on the circumstances. No wonder the body of literature around the phrase is considered "mountainous"—this is a matter of *survival*. Closing out the citation, there is the suave conjunction of "belief and action." If only the connections between thought and action were so simple as to be causal! But as Marx once shrewdly pointed out, "one does not judge an individual by what he thinks about himself . . . but, on the contrary, this consciousness must be explained from the contradictions of material life" (6). In other words, just because teaching is conducted under the explicit rubric of critical thinking, it cannot be taken as a given that expected results will have occurred. Rather, students' actions in the world will tell you if critical thinking has taken place. This poses problematic parameters for assessment, to say the least. (Incidentally, such an all-encompassing field of learning may begin to sound like more than college professors signed on for.)

If the stated imperatives of critical thinking do not necessarily render anything real in the world, anything remembered, then critical thinking can amount to mere mental exercise, a sensation that wisps away like the fading afterglow of a brisk walk or bike ride. The metaphor of a physical workout is more than simply convenient. As I puzzled over the phrase further, I asked my composition and rhetoric colleague Katherine Adams for her suggested reading, and she directed me to John Bean's seminal work *Engaging Ideas: The Professor's Guide to Integrating Writing, Critical Thinking, and Active Learning in the Classroom*, first published in 1996 and republished in subsequent editions. (I frequently find copies of the book in the freebies pile in my department's main office—I'm not sure what that means, if anything.)

Bean's study launches from the basic assumption that humans are naturally problem-solving creatures: "Presenting students with problems . . . taps into something natural and self-fulfilling in our beings" (2). Citing Ken Bain, Bean asserts, "'beautiful problems' create a 'natural critical learning environment'" (2). As Bean goes on to claim, "Part of the difficulty of teaching critical thinking, therefore, is awakening students to the existence of problems all around them" (2). The aesthetic terms and environmental rhetoric in these sentences are striking. They hint at a Nietzschean philosophy, with overtones of self-fulfillment and awakening in a raw, natural environment. As if to reinforce this ambient attitude, Bean goes on to elaborate: "As Brookfield (1987) claims, critical thinking is 'a productive and positive' activity. 'Critical thinkers are actively engaged with life.' This belief in the natural, healthy, and motivating pleasure of problems—and in the power of well-designed problems to awaken and stimulate the passive and unmotivated student—is one of the underlying premises of this book" (2).

Is this really what people are referring to when they speak of *critical thinking* in college? Can educators so easily justify course design and instruction—not to mention the entire project of the liberal arts—with recourse to active engagement with life, to what is "natural, healthy, and motivating?" In short, do people really envision higher education as a climb up a steep mountain? It sounds outright Romantic. Unfortunately, these platitudes may fail to satisfy measures of "value-added" and "return on investment" that colleges are under growing pressure to determine and demonstrate. Nevertheless, critical thinking lingers as an imprecise skill and pedantic requirement on college campuses.

For example, during a meeting for a strategic planning committee I was serving on at my university around this time, one of my colleagues adamantly rejected the inclusion of an allegedly trendy catchphrase ("experiential learning") as part of our mission statement, and insisted instead that we use the words "critical thinking." My colleague was ostensibly rejecting the professionalization of college education, in favor of the more properly *academic* priority of intellect. I understand this, and generally support my colleague's pushback. This preference, however, struck me as curious as it revealed that "critical thinking"—whatever cluster of ideas or intellectual ideals hide behind the phrase—had itself become something for which we were beginning to feel nostalgia. I had been in meetings before where *critical thinking* was the buzzword to be scoffed at. Now we were pining for this still amorphous thing, in its apparent recession, however elusive a definition remains.

As philosopher Margret Grebowicz has observed, "whatever is vernacular is what is most difficult to view from a critical distance" (19). The phrase "critical thinking" would seem to be caught in a double bind, its first word trapped in the very vernacular mist that such mental effort is supposed to dispel. The most authoritative definitions are either vast beyond usefulness, or brazen in their deferrals to romantic sentiments. Either way, critical thinking seems to point toward some immeasurable beyond: to a place where life is vibrant and rife with problems begging to be solved on the spot.

The Grebowicz line is from a book called *The National Park to Come*, which ends up being surprisingly applicable to the discussion at hand. At one point in this book Grebowicz analyzes historical constructions and critiques of "the scene of Nature" (with a capital N), suggesting, "what remains to be theorized is the wilderness hallucination, the postcard projection, the scenic backdrop, the wild as spectacle" (31). This is akin to the problem with the liberal arts broadly, the phrase "critical thinking" serving as a miniature version of this problem. Higher education is increasingly expected to be a concentrated site for focused job training and career preparation, which comes with the attendant fantasy of a robust economy and ample employment opportunities awaiting freshly minted graduates. This is one kind of "hallucination," to use Grebowicz's term. On the other hand, college can be imagined as a fecund (or vibrant, anyway) wilderness of sorts, life-generating and adventurous. This is the "scenic backdrop" behind Bean's formulation of critical thinking.

Such a conceived vista may be well-intentioned and even motivating from pedagogical and learning standpoints, but we would do well to recognize that these two governing fantasies—the wilderness of college, and a well-ordered economy beyond—are not only incompatible: they are also both *fantasies*, projections of something that can only be maintained as such. Critical thinking, in either context—as a practical skill geared to organized society *or* as a rugged comportment toward the ineffable—would seem to function as a third-order fantasy, hovering above the very things that we cannot come to terms with in a satisfying way: the role of liberal arts in higher education, in relation to a "real world" that operates according to fixed principles. This is a problem worthy of critical thinking, a knot that won't be severed by any ready blade or mere mental exercise, especially in our age of post-truth.

Unsettling place

The reader may have noticed by now that my interests in the work of literature are thoroughly entangled with my interests in place and space. These are big topics that can seem to have little connection to literature per se. As I was working on this book I found myself on a phone call with a *New York Times* reporter who had some questions for me about how social media was used at airports. The reporter became flustered at one point, trying to understand how my position as an English professor connected with my interests in airports. I explained how my experiences of working at an airport when I was starting graduate school were later inflected by my encounters with airports in American literature. In other words, my understanding of airports is shaped duly by practical inhabitance and literary and philosophical interpretation. The reporter didn't seem to be buying it, and grew more incredulous that such a connection might usefully exist between such different things: intellectual pursuits and practical transit considerations. (Not surprisingly, nothing came of that interview—the reporter ended the call abruptly, and when the article came out a few months later, it was a milquetoast account of how airlines can be summoned for customer service needs by using their Twitter handles.)

Part of the misunderstanding, I think, had to do with my own sense of language and representation as an environmental register—as things that reveal ecological sensibilities. And I view airports this way, too: as a site that exposes some of our most ingrained habits and assumptions with respect to living (together) on the planet. For me, then, communication is always about where it's taking place, too.

How else to explain this convergence, and what might it have to do with post-truth? One answer hinted at throughout this book so far could be that the work of literature is *grounding* in a special way. One problem with this, though, is that it is hard to orchestrate or predict how and when it's going to happen. Another problem is that is starts to sound like that hazy, environmental definition of critical thinking as a wilderness activity. I find myself walking a fine line between advocating a uselessly voluminous sense of *environment* and *place*, and wanting very specific, grounded accounts of our practices, and how we as a species are attentive to ecosystems (or not). I am interested in *unsettling* place, if then to take our place in space more seriously, carefully.

One June morning in 2017 I drove from my home in northern Michigan to Detroit, to attend the conference of the Association for the Study of Literature and Environment, and I arrived just in time to attend a plenary reading by the poet Ross Gay. I was rattled from the four-and-a-half-hour drive into the motor city, toward the end surrounded by menacing Buicks. I was not really in conference mode yet—hardly excited to think about literature *or* environment, to be honest. But I made my way to the large auditorium where the reading was to take place, and even hovered for a few moments outside, unsure of whether I should actually go in or not.

Finally I crossed the threshold and I settled into a seat in the back of a packed auditorium as Christoph Irmscher introduced the poet, and then Gay's reading commenced. Leery and tired at first, I was gradually drawn into the poems from Gay's book *A Catalog of Unabashed Gratitude*, and delighted by his preview of a book in progress called "Delights": short essays written about daily delights, one written each day for a year. The effect of this reading on me was grounding, even as it shuttled me into distant places and remote sensations. Gay's reading was powerful, animated, and sincere—his poems reflected the work of literature at its best, grounding the audience even as they sent us on flights of fancy and into distant realms of thought and empathy.

Obviously we cannot live in an ongoing state of poetry readings, but I think that this experience can have ripple effects and far reaching consequences. It is about listening for what one is unprepared for, about being open to unexpected syntheses. It's about being in a place together, in truth sometimes an unsettling place—for the reader as much as the audience—as a way to practice social (and ecological) being-together on vaster scales and in other contexts. It's not about getting at Truth, but about pushing through the mush of post-truth to an unsettled place of patient listening and interaction.

David Foster Wallace: Don't believe the hype

As I've intimated throughout this book, one of the more troubling champions of such a mode of patient communication—and higher education, as a focused context for this—is someone who had a difficult time surviving it himself: David Foster Wallace. I've mentioned my seminar on Wallace a few times already, and it's a topic with which I have a fraught relationship. Students get excited about this course, and request it in the years that I don't offer it. But I'm not sure I am going to teach it again. The seminar feels too monolithic, and too misleading. If I am interested in the preservation of the liberal arts as a model of higher education, I am equally suspicious of traditional notions of authorship as well as the culture that fuels and subtends such notions of individual greatness.

There is a clever scene in the closing minutes of James Ponsoldt's *The End of the Tour*, when Wallace (played by Jason Segel) is out in his driveway scraping snow and ice off his Honda Civic. Meanwhile, David Lipsky (played by Jesse Eisenberg) inside Wallace's house furtively takes last-minute notes as he makes his final observations at the end of his stint accompanying Wallace on book tour. At one point Lipsky enters a nearly pitch-black room, and we see a ray of light wash over Wallace's writing desk: we get a glimpse of a well-used personal computer, a notepad and pen, crammed bookshelves against the wall. It is the wish image of a writer's sacred den, a domestic shrine that emanates the residual aura of the Author at work. It strikes me that this is one of the things some viewers *wanted* from this movie, and maybe what they want from David Foster Wallace in general: the architectural plans, and the supply list and tools, for *writing*—for really *being* a certain kind of writer. Of course it's just a fleeting peek at this inner sanctum, and we sense that the movie is wrapping up at this point, soon to fade out.

I saw this film on a Saturday morning in New York City the day after it opened. The theater wasn't crowded at all. The vibe was mellow and subdued. I chuckled several times throughout the film, but I didn't hear anyone else laughing. The experience was like sipping warm Earl Grey tea while someone tells you a long and sometimes unintentionally funny story in a comfortable (if kind of awkward) living room. I watched the movie with my former student Stewart Sinclair, who had since moved to the city. Stewart is working hard to become a writer—I mean to really *be* a full-time writer, and I sincerely believe he has what it takes. Just two nights before the film, we had workshopped his essay "The Slaughter," a piece that overtly grapples with and extends David Foster Wallace's classic essay "Consider the Lobster." Stewart was in my David Foster Wallace seminar at Loyola University New Orleans the first time I taught that class, in 2011; Wallace is one of the writers who inspired Stewart to want to write, and to think critically about the world. So it made sense that we should go to *The End of the Tour* together, when the timing serendipitously worked out. I had considered seeing the film the night before, with a few friends, as Wallace kept coming up in conversation over dinner. In the end, we were all too tired, and we dispersed to continue our own ordinary lives. But so Wallace was in the air—and there were a lot of opinions, attitudes, and emotions swirling around *The End of the Tour*.

Here's the thing: *The End of the Tour* is a well-made film. It has solid acting, nicely detailed regional touches (Joan Cusack in a Ford station wagon *is* Minnesota), and tense moments that are deftly handled from a cinematic perspective. It is also a movie of ideas, as Steve Zeitchik noted in the *LA Times*. It raises for consideration some (if not all) of the central concerns of David Foster Wallace's writing: existential loneliness, the threats of increasingly immersive technologies, and the risks of constant entertainment, rampant consumerism, and celebrity culture. Nothing in the movie breaks from the overt themes of Wallace's actual writings—unless you want to go meta and insist that the movie itself is everything Wallace would have *hated*. But then, the joke is on us, too, as in one scene Wallace, Lipsky, and friends sit in a familiar looking theater watching a movie, and we all sort of gaze obliquely at one another for a few strange moments.

But what struck me as Stewart and I watched the film was just how ordinary it all was: the movie, the treatment of the characters, the airport scenes, the car rental lots, the appetites temporarily satisfied with junk food, the outbursts and mumblings. There is a scene in which Lipsky practically begs Wallace to admit he's brilliant, and Wallace rebuffs him. Wallace values his "regular-guyness" not as an affectation but as a survival tactic, and as a sincere reality. This is a reality (and not just of being a writer) that we are reticent to admit or openly embrace: no one escapes the ordinariness of everyday life; no one escapes being regular. No one. Sure, there are moments (at widely different scales) of excitement, passion, genius, violence, and rage, there are inequities and injustices that are horrible and that we (hopefully) work to address or redress. But these are all set against a profoundly mundane backdrop—really the overwhelming foreground—of ordinary life. Wallace's writings wiggle into the ordinary, the regular, even when his topics occasionally appear charged or esoteric at first blush. But then, too, *writing* is ordinary. It's just a life, just a form of living life.

Two of the most common complaints about *The End of the Tour* were A) Wallace would NEVER have approved of or been comfortable with the movie, and therefore it should not have been made, or B) Jason Segel didn't do an accurate job of representing Wallace—it's a caricature, a greatly exaggerated animation of the Author's tics and foibles. These objections often followed one another, but they are something of a contradiction: presumably, if Segel had captured Wallace *perfectly*, or if the casting had been different and preferred, the role would be more permissible? On the other hand, if one truly believes on principle that the film *should not have been made at all*, then there is nothing to talk about in terms of the film itself. It should be a conversation stopper. Instead, it's a floodgate. If we want to talk about the film, well then we enter into complex topics such as the work of art, the politics of representation, the society of the spectacle, and so forth. And IF we want to talk about art, we can make no easy judgments, segmentations, or prioritizations between the film and the novel, the fiction and the nonfiction, the life and the death. We have to plunge in.

I've witnessed some of the intellectual gymnastics, interpretive tendencies, and gut responses that contribute to the turmoil around this latest incarnation of Wallace. My students (and I should say that in this seminar they are usually approximately 50/50 female/male, and not just white) tend to come to the class as fans, or incredibly leery of Wallace, or sometimes somewhere in between: neutral, genuinely curious (their older sister or brother used to lug around a tattered copy of *Infinite Jest*). Whichever way, my students share a desire to know what the deal is with this writer: Was he *really* a genius? If so, can we beat him at his own clever games? (Out-write him, out-critique him—at the very least, outlive him?) And if he's not the genius he's cracked up to be, why not, and what's the hype all about then? Should we believe the hype?

Let's go back to Wallace's short story "Incarnations of Burned Children." As I learned from my students, this story is apparently a staple of some introductory creative writing courses. So what is it about "Incarnations of Burned Children" that beginning writers are supposed to learn? How to create detached perspective, sentence pacing, narrative suspense, offbeat description—*writerly* things, things having to do with writing about the world, writing *in* the world, writing the world. How to tell a story. The story itself is allegedly about childhood trauma and the ripple effects of family, culture, modern life—ripple effects that reverberate both directions, in and out. But as a piece of writing it's something taken also to be an inspiration *to write*. Wallace was a writer. Wallace taught writing, and his writings continue to generate more writing: as homage and in admiration, as literary criticism and history, and now as an oblique form of reflexive cultural critique: what would *he* think of this movie? And does that even matter?

One question we have to back up and ask is whether this movie about Wallace will encourage people to write. Indeed, it has already prompted numerous responses in prose (see the incisive reviews, reflections, and reactions by Anna Shechtman, David Edelstein, A. O. Scott, Glenn Kenny, Mike Miley, Hannah Gersen, Jason Tanz: the list goes on). If all this writing is not exactly like Wallace's in style or form, is it at least in a similar critical vein, or probing spirit, raising questions of media, writing, self-awareness, irony, and so on? And if so, what's the problem exactly? To put it bluntly: what do we want from Wallace, if not avid further engagement with thinking and writing?

Yet if we *do* want to do justice to Wallace's actual writing, don't we need to think a bit more flexibly—I almost want to say *dialectically*—about fiction and nonfiction about these things in tension called authors, stories, movies, and, well, contemporary life? If Wallace provides us with one useful tool, isn't it an unsettling device, like a hammer claw for the brain, or pliers for the thorns of the mind? Where we think things are nailed down and sealed tight, or forever stuck and lodged in, they're really not, or shouldn't be. We must loosen our most deeply held assumptions, our habits of thought and action. If we have our minds made up about the accuracies or inaccuracies of *The End of the Tour*, its pure motives or ill intents, aren't we falling into just the sort of hermeneutic trap that Wallace would point out and (however quietly or circuitously) decry?

In his 1969 essay "What is an Author?" Michel Foucault proposed the following: "Writing unfolds like a game that invariably goes beyond its own rules and transgresses its limits. In writing, the point is not to manifest or exalt the act of writing, nor is it to pin a subject within language; it is, rather, a question of creating a space into which the writing subject constantly disappears" (206). In *The End of the Tour*, the maximalist novel *Infinite Jest* seems to exert this gravitational pull—both on the author as well as on readers and potentially predatory journalists. As an act of *writing*, it has this slippery quality that galls Lipsky *and* Wallace alike: as much as the great novel exists as a concrete thing in the world, it has also gone viral, and has mutated somehow—the novel cannot be pinned down, least of all by its author. It's prescient of our age of post-truth.

If *Infinite Jest* in part is an elaborate experiment that submerges film and film criticism in the deep pool of a novel, might it not be OK to have a film that tries to flood the screen with the work(s) of a writer? If it were just a fictional writer, maybe. But, as Roland Barthes claimed just before Foucault's essay in 1967, "To give a text an Author is to impose a limit on that text, to furnish it with a final signified, to close the writing" (147). Because Wallace has attained the status of a big "A" author—someone with clear intentions, who wrote with utter decisiveness (so the legend goes)—this creates all sorts of trouble for the film, which must at every turn wrest itself from the clutches of this monolithic entity, the Author—this entity which is actually a *void*. Barthes articulated "the death of the Author"—letting go of the fantasy of authorial singularity—as a radical break, unleashing the interpretive and creative potential of readers. And while Wallace may certainly have believed that there is always a living author at the nexus of any text (somewhat amending Barthes), he would probably have readily admitted the unstoppable dissemination of the written text (and the Author in tow), too. Wallace was in on these debates, as is manifest in his review essay "Greatly Exaggerated." So if we take Wallace seriously, including his working knowledge of the late-60s and onward poststructuralist theories of the Author, there should be nothing surprising or appalling about *The End of the Tour*. It is a ready-made extension of Wallace's writing and thinking in more than one sense.

I went into *The End of the Tour* with teaching writing in mind. The subsequent semester I was scheduled to teach a class I'd never taught before, Introduction to Creative Writing. Such a class may sound basic enough, but even the beginning writer is bound to suddenly and unwittingly stumble into the thorny brambles of celebrity authorship, the vexed relationship between writing privately and having a public persona, and the maelstrom of publishing in the digital age. These matters are interesting to me on a philosophical level, and they offer important lessons and pose puzzles for students who want to become writers. I appreciated the brief scene toward the beginning of *The End of the Tour* where we see Segel's Wallace teaching his creative writing class at Illinois State University—it looked pretty genuine, almost real. I know it's just a movie, but the unpretentiousness of this scene was impressive. There is a strange continuum here, with the humble, humdrum college writing classroom on one end, and (a movie about) a high-profile public book tour and slick reportage on the other end. On the one side, you have ordinary life and regular people trying to communicate in earnest; on the other side, you have big deals, fast talkers, expense accounts, and the near total commodification of art. Perhaps David Foster Wallace—as a writer, and as a subject of fascination—touches so many nerves because he can be charted, mapped, and trapped at various points across this continuum.

To say Wallace could never have anticipated and/or would never have approved of a cinematic depiction of himself seems to underestimate or outright miss Wallace's own insights about commercialism, screen culture, and our penchant for entertainment. Wallace may or may not have "liked" the movie (also, these things can change!), but I don't think he would have been surprised in the least to see the ways that his Author-function has attained notoriety in the wake of his death. Had Kierkegaard been around to consider the case of Wallace, he might have written a book called *The Screening Unto Death*. Wallace was well familiar with literary fame and the more artistic ambitions of indie film, as well as their occasional coincidences, interminglings, and bumpings up against one another. Look at the very short story "Death is Not the End": Wallace represents an accomplished poet/Author as an object of spectation and as abject human embodiment, simultaneously. Consider the character of David Wallace in *The Pale King* who "becomes a creature of the system" (547), which Anna Shechtman employed smartly to end her essay "David Foster Wallace's Closed Circuit." See how Wallace turned a movie set rather inside out and into a hilariously intricate panoramic essay in "David Lynch Keeps His Head." Are we that far from the very preoccupations and fascinations that comprise Wallace's own writings? It's possible that Wallace may be rolling in his grave about *The End of the Tour*; it's also possible that he's simply rolling his eyes, nodding along with us—maybe even snickering.

If I were to offer my seminar again, I'd likely teach this film in order to discuss all these things that are entangled with the hype around Wallace. But I can't see teaching it, not yet. Not when we have another monomaniacal author figure to deal with: our president and all the fantasies that attend him.

Maggie Nelson's *The Argonauts*:
A book review that is not one

Nine years prior to writing this book, I was finishing up my doctoral work at the University of California, Davis. I had written a dissertation about airports in American literature and culture; I was demonstrating my PhD's "designated emphasis" in critical theory, applying concepts of postmodern identity, the production of space, and semiotic indeterminacy to a range of primary texts. At the same time, I was pushing against some of the more tedious strictures of the genre of the doctoral dissertation—even in the most simple way, by titling my thesis "Airport Reading" and refusing to provide a lengthy, jargon-flinging, name-dropping subtitle after a colon.

Seven years later, I would find myself on the verge of a semester in which I would teach a creative nonfiction workshop, followed a few hours later by a course on critical theory. I find myself increasingly spread between these two subfields of the discipline of English: one of them in-your-face experimental and risking an "anything goes" mentality; the other very much entrenched (although it does not like to think of itself in such a way) in certain names, ideas, foundational texts, and methods deemed of value in the service of revaluating all values. Often creative writing and literary criticism are seen as distant (and sometimes downright oppositional) ends on the strange micro-spectrum that is the discipline of English. Occasionally these two poles collapse and smash together, and the results can be jarring or thrilling, or both.

Maggie Nelson's 2015 book *The Argonauts* bridges this divide, or troubles it—or perhaps bridging it *is* troubling it. It's thrilling and jarring. To summarize that the book is about the fluidity of sexual identity would be to seize on only one part of the book; Nelson is really interested in all manner of transitions that together, messily and lusciously, become human experience. Sampling everything from gender bending to being stalked, from making art to mundane acts of parenting, from birthing to passing, and from desire to death, Nelson dispenses with any stable center point from which the author might knowingly, authoritatively *settle things*.

The book is also about *writing*. Nelson pulls back the curtain to expose an unseemly writing process, and in so doing the book deftly deflates its own author-ego, even as it is of course asserted over the course of each page. *The Argonauts* is relentlessly aware of its linguistic fabrications, bearing it all in direct prose while reminding the reader that, for instance, "One must also become alert to the multitude of possible uses, possible contexts, the wings with which each word can fly" (8). The book is a cobbled together and sometimes capricious seeming performance—a project that disavows its own coherence, its own necessary attempt at resolution.

And yet, what we have in the end *is* a book: probably around 45,000 words of exploration, rumination, and meditation—all appearing under the covering cipher of *The Argonauts*. If the book seems at once sprawling in its subject and arbitrarily limited, this would seem to fulfill the promise of the title, as something that retains identity even as it shifts material components and shape.

The book is littered with ultra-minimal citations in the form of names dropped in the margins, usually (but not always) corresponding with *an italicized sort-of-quotation*. It's an attempt to cite-without-citing, a grasp at loosely appropriating while also flagging, or paying *just enough* homage via callouts rather than by scrupulous footnotes. I found this tactic distracting and vaguely annoyingly, at first; it felt like name-dropping, as if these spectral figures were supposed to be assuring me of Nelson's academic street cred. Julia Kristeva, Judith Butler, Eve Sedgwick, Michel Foucault—I get it, you went to grad school, you've studied the cool cats. But maybe I'm just being a jerk; I didn't really feel that way, all the time. I could appreciate these sparse anchor points from another angle: they held down the text, a text that could at times seem to be floating away. And if they made me wonder about the provenance or context of each quasi-citation, isn't this perfectly fine, and potentially productive? In my book *The End of Airports* I did something similar with aphoristic lines drawn from other writers, sans citation; it might be experienced as irritating, but my wager was that it would spark intellectual adventure. I like to think that Nelson made a similar gamble with *The Argonauts'* oblique references.

Still, the text does drift. Sometimes it feels like the nearly unedited transcripts of a journal, entries jumping around in time or associatively in ways that make the reader struggle to connect the dots. At one point Nelson tells the reader that she used her marginalia from graduate school texts as fodder to create poems. Recycling is in the air. In certain points *The Argonauts* almost resembles a seasoned blog stripped of context and reproduced as a book—indeed, even the paragraph breaks absent of indents bear this formal trace, of the look of prose writing in our age of post-truth. And while Nelson alludes to qualms concerning online hyper-communication, the book is nevertheless entangled with digital media from the first pages—Google beckons.

Lest this make the book sound sloppy, Nelson is acutely aware of the multimedia tapestry being woven in *The Argonauts*. What makes Nelson's project work so well is how it shuttles relentlessly between forms, genres, even audiences. At times I was frustrated that *The Argonauts* seemed to be demanding too much homework from lay readers, while at other times Nelson risked playing too fast and loose for academic readers. But maybe these are the cardinal virtues of Nelson's book, risks that both "creative writers" and "critical theorists" could learn from. I certainly did. Because, really, do we need the ridiculous appellations "creative writer" and "critical theorist?" How do writers get slotted into such narrow conceptions and slapped with such counterproductive labels?

I started writing about this book autobiographically, and for a reason. As I read *The Argonauts* I marveled at Nelson's agile moves between high theoretical concepts and sincere personal reflection. I found myself thinking back on my own graduate studies, and all of the skilled writers I met who were, for better or worse, being corralled into this or that type of writing, *creative* or *critical*. What an unfortunate and false choice! And truth be told, it was not even that bad at UC Davis, where graduate students had (at least it seemed to me) plenty of latitude in terms of style, approach, method, voice, and form. I learned as much from the "writers" as I did from the "critics," and there was a lot of mutual respect across these two parts of the department.

But still, this dichotomy has been institutionalized at large, and I hear it perpetuated all too often. Someone will say, "Oh yeah, so and so is working on a collection of stories, *but first* they *have to* publish their dissertation book!" Or, "Well yes I write nonfiction, but I *have to* finish my *novel* in order to get tenure." *This* kind of book versus *that* kind of book; a Platonic publisher fawning after a mythical monograph; the blustery winds of a certain "next book project" that would obviously be a fit for a certain Big Name Press. And worse, these mini-narratives are often bandied about *before anything has really even been written!*

What have we done to writing? How did these awkward categories come to so tightly regulate—and often snuff out—the creative *and* critical fire that, finally, has to be burning beneath any writer who simply wants to write a book? This is a well-trod debate, for sure, and one we often wisely avoid, for fear of falling down a rabbit hole that turns into a many branching subterrane of disciplinary history and pointless spats between literary icons and condescending critics. But *The Argonauts* got me thinking anew about the terms of this debate—critics versus (or qua) writers—and thinking too that we may be in a new era with respect to this divide: it may be finally eroding, or showing new stress fractures, anyway.

The Argonauts made me think about the books that might be written if many scholars/writers were not bound by idiosyncratic and capricious so-called standards or genre conventions of scholarship and publication. I finished the last pages of Nelson's book wishing there were *more* books like this—which is admittedly an awkward thing to think in relation to a book that struck me again and again as so excellently *singular*. Still, I found myself thinking about various writer/critic friends, thinking "*So and so could write a great book like this!*"—"like this" meaning the hybrid nature of *autotheory* that Nelson has mastered, but that we recognize in the works of Roland Barthes, Virginia Woolf, Susan Sontag, and somewhat rare others who occupy the bizarre canon of criticism.

In this vein, *The Argonauts* also caused me to reflect on why Ian Bogost and I came up with our series Object Lessons. Ian and I wanted to create a venue for writers to write in their own ways, for wide audiences, about things that interested them. This may sound terribly loose and unfocused, but it turns out to be anything but. Object Lessons books demand a kind of intensity of attention, constraint, and concision that makes their titular objects pop into focus, replete with cyclonic inner lives and extending forms that take shape on the page. When I first read Maggie Nelson's *Bluets* a few years ago, I remember thinking that it could have been an Object Lessons book, that *this* was what I envisioned for the series: it was refreshingly short, captivatingly personal, and full of sincere wonder. *Bluets* showed me what Object Lessons books could do—a standard of delightful unpredictability and concentration, together.

I'm losing the thread here. Or maybe not. Anyway, I warned the reader that this was a book review that is not one. But to close more or less on the book in question: *The Argonauts* got me thinking about why we write, and why we write *what* we write. And *who* we write *for*. These are topics that you'd think we'd keep in mind—"we" being writing instructors—but I think we lose sight of these things all too often. Do we write for readers? Who do we imagine our readers to be? Do we sometimes write for readers yet to come? How should we keep these questions in mind as we actually, really, *write*?

So what am I going to do with Maggie Nelson's *The Argonauts*? Teach it as a jumping off point (a "perch," to use Nelson's word) for future creative nonfiction workshops? Or assign it as a deliciously messy concluding text for my critical theory courses? Could I do both? And then, what about it as it relates to my own writing? Will I take Nelson's cue and join her "ongoing song" of curiosity, critique, and care for the strangeness of life? Yes, I will.

Don DeLillo's *Zero K*: When does the person become the body?

A few years ago one of my students wrote a senior thesis on Don DeLillo, covering the themes, contexts, and philosophical issues that run through the contemporary author's novels across several decades. This spring I received a letter in my campus mailbox from this student, with a newspaper clipping about DeLillo's latest novel *Zero K*, as well as a handwritten note that said, "Looking forward to this. Probably the last one we can expect from him?" I flinched and thought to myself, *Well that puts it rather morbidly*.

But once I had read *Zero K*, and been washed over—more, baptized—by the publicity campaign surrounding the novel, my former student's assessment didn't seem quite so bleak. The novel is itself a meditation on death and something like its obverse, the fetishization of eternal life. Gushing lines of praise adorning the book seem to almost eulogize DeLillo, as if this novel is to serve as a small if multitudinous cenotaph, hundreds of thousands of little paper gravestones in bookstores and on bookshelves, maybe even on people's bedside tables. Martin Amis lauded the book accordingly: "The gods have equipped DeLillo with the antennae of a visionary." *ELLE* summoned the author's entire oeuvre to claim, "Reading DeLillo's books bolsters our belief in the art of fiction." The *Houston Chronicle* posited that DeLillo "understands the capacity of words to elevate us above the mundane."

Gods, belief, elevation—this is nothing short of a religious encounter, forced upon the reader before the cover is even cracked. My friend Ian ordered *Zero K* but felt so set upon by the overwhelming acclaim that he was unable to read the book, and he ended up returning it to Amazon. At one point Ian told me he wanted the book out of his house. Only an object endowed with mystical qualities might have such an effect.

Sadly—or thankfully, depending on your perspective—reading the actual book doesn't deliver quite such an experience. In fact, what DeLillo has always been good at is puncturing these sorts of overtures, often uttered by his characters only to be deflated precisely *by* the mundane. And *Zero K*, too, revels in the mundane—at least, it does some of the time. We find ourselves in the pockets of one character, to consider the careful placement of handkerchief in relation to keys, the bulk of a wallet and the repetitive feel of its presence as gauged by the minor tap of the palm. We linger on an ATM machine, with its curious admixture of social and private rituals. A monk is seen to be wearing black and white gym sneakers beneath the hem of his robe.

Unfortunately, these material details of the everyday are subordinated to the heavier topics of the novel: in short, a near-future sort of looming apocalypticism and the corollary behaviors of humans who entertain and are entertained by death, at turns. This is all fine and good, and not entirely out of line with other DeLillo novels such as *The Names* and *Point Omega*, among others. But in *Zero K* the story lines are either too fragmentary or too tunneled into minutiae—they never quite come together in the way they could. A great novelist does not necessarily make a great novel. But, to adapt one of DeLillo's own questions in *Zero K*, "when does the person become the body [of work]?" When an anticipated novel warrants a sidebar ad in the *New Yorker* magazine, riding on previous successes and wagered against a new (possibly last, potentially *not as good*) work of fiction, readers beware. It is no small irony that a novel allegedly exploring the culmination of a successful life and its inevitable ruin should then resurrect an uncannily similar dynamic around the novel's author, and the novel as an ur-object of art.

It is as if the book's publisher needed *Zero K* to be the bedrock that firmed up, once and for all, DeLillo's reputation (and marketability) as a novelist (with a robust backlist, of course). Meanwhile, *Zero K* weighs the differences and similarities between life and death, a person and a rock, art and medium, fabulous wealth and bare asceticism. The book is at least hinting at—if not outright advocating—a certain arbitrariness that exists between these various seemingly clear-cut terms.

Has the publisher not read the book? Or have they simply decided to go whole hog into the very realm of postmodern irony that DeLillo himself has for so long written about with astonishing insight and sophisticated awareness? If so, this might be the paradigmatic novel for an age of post-truth.

I understand that DeLillo is just a person, too, with bills to pay. Of course it was time for him to publish a new book, which he has now done. But I have to wonder: is the author at all bothered by the manic reproduction of some of the very things that *Zero K* (and other novels of his) are trying to slow down and think about, dare I say *critique*? Of course this line of questioning gets uncomfortable quickly. I want my publisher to market my books as best they can, too; who am I to judge? Let's get back to the proper business of literary criticism, the work of literature.

As I finished the novel I felt like it either should have been edited down to short story length (which it was, in a sense, when it appeared in the *New Yorker* earlier as "Sine Cosine Tangent"), or it could have been fleshed out into a maximalist novel—developing the characters, following some of the threads further—and thereby potentially granting it status alongside DeLillo's great novel of the mid-90s, *Underworld* (not to mention maybe even David Foster Wallace's *Infinite Jest*). Incidentally, the publisher's bold print on the back cover of my advance reader's copy of *Zero K* asserts that it is his "finest novel since *Underworld*." This seems utterly bizarre to me, since both *Cosmopolis* and *Falling Man* are forceful, extremely shrewd novels chronicling turn-of-the-century tensions and terrors. And *Point Omega*, in many ways, covers similar material as does *Zero K*, but in much tighter form. So for the publisher to brush over these three novels and equate *Zero K* with *Underworld* seems reckless—and not particularly generous to the author, either.

There are some delightful passages in *Zero K*, and the concepts are compelling, if not altogether original at times. The TV screens that play looped images of horrific scenes seem pulled right out of Wallace's story "The Suffering Channel." DeLillo recycles the phrase "dead time" from his earlier novel *The Names*—but outside the context of an airport, it doesn't cut quite as sharply. There is in fact a nice paragraph about airport routines in *Zero K*, but it seems to rehearse what *Valparaiso* got at much more playfully, if also more darkly. One of my favorite lines in the book occurs when the main character contemplates the fate of his stepmother, who has been cryogenically preserved for future rebirth: "Does she know she's waiting? Is she wait-listed?" Here is DeLillo at his finest, piercing an existential quandary with the everyday jargon of commercial air travel. (This is also a nice example of what I call *airportness*: the cluster of sensations, narratives, and protocols that define modern flight, and how single objects, images, or phrases can conjure the entire menagerie of air travel.)

In the end, *Zero K* left me with a sense of vague dissatisfaction, but I think this has much more to do with the hysteria around the book-as-event, and less to do with the novel itself. The novel is a journey, and if it is frustrating, that's actually OK because the story is about contemporary frustrations with the (mis)adventure of modern human progress. It's almost like the final, fractured piece in a trilogy that would include *Cosmopolis* and *Point Omega*, gathering a few new characters and their trajectories into the oscillating mix. But the ancillary social text—the genuflecting around DeLillo, the very making of the Author into a body, a statue not unlike the haunting visage on the novel's cover—this is what is ultimately disappointing. It's as if we've learned nothing from DeLillo over all these years from all his wonderful, *critical* fiction.

Thirty observations after reading Sarah Manguso's *300 Arguments*

I've been interested in aphorisms for a long time, though I've struggled to actually write them myself.

Sarah Manguso's new book of aphorisms *300 Arguments* is the best example of this genre I've experienced since reading Nietzsche in college. Yet saying it like that makes the genre sound like a coherent thing, which it is not. It also makes it sound *developmental*.

Collections of aphorisms are hardly a growth sector: bookstores don't dedicate sections to this genre. But a college course on aphorisms increasingly strikes me as a good idea.

Aphorisms can seem to build logically, like a Wittgenstein argument. But just when you think you're approaching a clear thesis or resolution, there shouldn't be one—which should always come as a surprise.

Gertrude Stein's *Tender Buttons* are a forebear of any decent attempt at aphorisms: not because they make sense, but because they keep going and going. A worthy accumulation comes to embody its own method.

Should aphorisms be personal? Or should they seek a sort of universal subject? It depends on what you mean by *personal*, and what you mean by *universal*.

The thing about aphorisms is that they can be only so good and still hang together. Anything more than that and they'll break apart.

Aphorisms and tautologies are like college roommates who never met before moving in together: they can complement each other and even turn into best friends, or they can just coexist in awkward tension. Of course, they can also become mortal enemies.

A confession within an aphorism functions like a fortune within a cookie. Which thing gets priority depends on multiple factors including prescience, staleness, context, and appetite.

Aphorisms revel in the general and nonspecific. But to be perceived as *true*, they must be attributable. We always want it both ways, and this goes far beyond aphorisms.

One time a college roommate purchased a huge container of fortune cookies for our house. It was an incredible deal, he said, from Sam's Club. But you rarely want to eat more than one fortune cookie at a time, two at most. So by the time we graduated, the giant see-through plastic container was still half full. We were tired of fortune cookies.

Can a bunch of aphorisms comprise a great book? Yes, especially when the aphorisms remain keenly aware of the container in which they will eventually arrive in the hands of the reader.

The only thing better than repetition is the only thing better than repetition.

Aphorisms excel at jumping across things that seem impossibly far apart. A philosophical problem? An opportunity for extrapolation?

Recently my mother wondered whether a certain poet always wrote about sex. I didn't know how to respond; there were obvious assumptions at play, like that the poet was probably a sex maniac.

But how much can we ever know about a writer, based on what they write?

A good book is hard to find. That's no aphorism; it's more like a short story.

A funny thing about aphorisms is how poorly most of them age. I'm curious to see how this applies to aphorisms that are explicitly about aging.

An enjoyable feature of aphorisms in books is their ability to respect and even utilize page breaks for effect. They only have so much room to make their points—or undo them.

Aphorisms *can* be broken up and continue after a page break, but they lose their *something*. Aphorisms thrive on the ineffable. And the ineffable needs boundaries in order to be just on the verge of being effed.

Sometimes we seek out parables, other times allegories. We almost never go looking for aphorisms. They come to us unbidden, and render us senseless.

Do we know how to read aphorisms? Do we know how to learn from aphorisms? There's no guidebook or "very short introduction" for this genre. That's kind of the point, isn't it? Ironic.

Should teachers be able to impart their lessons via aphorisms? If so, why all the extra exercises, elaborate assignments, and hours of instruction and reading? Yet if not, are the lessons even worth learning?

Opposites neither attract nor repel. They don't even exist in pure opposite form, really.

There are three kinds of books: but this kind of thinking won't help you read or write books, much less get along in everyday life.

Book reviews can attempt to hover above the work, or feign to report from a distance. But writing about writing is still writing.

The best aphorisms are about children, or are childlike. The worst aphorisms know too much. There, I said it.

The more an aphorism proclaims to relay truth, the sketchier it becomes.

A flash of illumination. The warming glow of wonder. The taillights of an aphorism receding in the rear view.

You can always make money, but you can never make time.

The limits of language are the minefield of aphorisms. Yes, and their playground.

Liberal arts: A safe space?

Scaling up slightly from aphorisms, there are short short stories, or flash fiction—these are some of my favorite types of texts to teach, as they can be read, reread, digested, and discussed over the course of one class period. These sorts of classes can reflect liberal arts at their best: everyone literally on the same page, while yet entertaining divergent ideas, hunches, and insights and sharing these things together. But it's hardly a formulaic pedagogy.

There's a short story by Lydia Davis called "Idea for a Sign" which explores the social dynamic of settings where people who don't know one another must sit side-by-side, as on a train. Davis suggests that it would be a whole lot easier if everyone wore signs explaining exactly what they will and will not do while sitting there, to facilitate maximum transparency and comfort while in close quarters. As you might expect, this prompt to bullet-point basic attributes and actions quickly becomes an absurd and untenable encyclopedic exercise in listing, as each tic, habit, and affect must be delineated and parsed, in advance, to the point that every "sign" becomes a long stream of prose. Each person is revealed to be no more—and no less—than a complex self, entangled in a densely social world. So much for the neat and tidy individual simply sitting on a train. It turns out that people are complicated, and that safe spaces are difficult to ensure.

While working on this book I was on a college committee charged with helping to define and articulate what we meant in a mission statement by the term "liberal arts." This may sound straightforward enough: is there anything to explain or justify beyond a basic commitment to knowledge across multiple core disciplines? A balance of science, mathematics, the arts, philosophy, history, literature, and language, it is a model of education that goes back quite a ways, rooted in Greco-Roman ideals that balance modes of inquiry and intellectual study.

We might venture a simple definition and say that liberal arts education cultivates *well-rounded individuals*. Unfortunately, the well-rounded individual turns out to be slippery to describe, much less keep hold of. It is like Lydia Davis's sign-wearer, a vortex for every possible behavior and characteristic. What "well-rounded" means depends on who is in the room, and valuing what, at any given moment. As anyone who has sat on a committee knows, these interests and values can shift wildly depending on who is sitting where, from meeting to meeting. Even the notoriously meta-sounding "committee on committees" on certain university campuses is hardly a neutral domain.

I've been thinking back on my own liberal arts education, which took place at that traditional small college in the Midwest. I've tried to understand what went on there, extrapolate what worked and what could work better. I remember one semester when I went directly from an astronomy class to medieval philosophy—my mind would be spinning at dinnertime, and usually well into the night. There were the three semesters of Latin: intensely difficult but also ineffably rewarding, working on basic Ovid translations. That stimulating biology class on Michigan flora. The small seminar on Nietzsche and Kierkegaard team-taught by four professors, one each from philosophy, English, psychology, and sociology. Discussing the complexities and subtleties of *Walden* in an American Literature course, then going on a backpacking trip with the professor, Dr. Pete Olson, who would become a great friend long after my college years were over. My liberal arts education acted as a sort of safe space for these cross-disciplinary forays and productive collisions.

Of course, there were also many uncataloged experiences and misadventures that occurred during my liberal arts education. These were all the wanderings, passions, attractions, predicaments, malaise, and uncomfortable encounters that also happen in college—the very experiences that college creates a time and space for. This is something that faculty members (not to mention administrators) do not like to talk about or include as part of the mission of a college: the messy time and space required for awkward mental developments and incremental personal growth. These are things that occur outside—though they often necessarily intersect with—the classroom, but which could not happen without the pretense of college: being away from family, living with peers in a dorm or similar setting, learning how to manage one's own time, work load, and so on.

In Josh Radnor's 2012 film *Liberal Arts*, one of the narrative arcs involves a minor character who goes from being a tortured, introspective soul, schlepping around a copy of David Foster Wallace's *Infinite Jest*, to an awakened spirit who might finally risk living in the world instead of in a book. Strangely enough, this conversion can be taken as a very distilled interpretation of

Wallace's own "philosophy" of life, as it was summed up by the end of the famous commencement speech he gave at Kenyon College in 2005 (coincidentally, Kenyon was where *Liberal Arts* was filmed).

According to Wallace, the real takeaway from a liberal arts education is at once ambitiously holistic and utterly humble: "It is about simple awareness—awareness of what is so real and essential, so hidden in plain sight all around us, that we have to keep reminding ourselves, over and over: 'This is water, this is water'" (143). It is about day-to-day consciousness in a world that constantly distracts and evades our grasp. It is also, arguably, a tactic that does not work very well: too much awareness may result in paralysis. It's one thing to give a motivational speech about being fully attentive, but it's another thing to live like this, particularly "in the day-to-day trenches of adult existence" (9), as Wallace puts it.

But why are we talking about life as if it is a battlefield? When we refer to being well-rounded in a liberal arts context, I don't think it means becoming like Emerson's detached, drone-like eyeball: "*I become a transparent eye-ball; I am nothing; I see all; the currents of the Universal Being circulate through me. . .*" (39). Taken too seriously this way, the well-rounded individual can be a repository for a kind of ruthless, rugged individualist—someone who confuses solipsism with sovereignty. Recall the nihilists in *The Big Lebowski* who claim to "believe in nothing," but who also whine, "*It's not fair!*" when they don't get their way.

What we mean by well-rounded in a more careful formulation might mean an acquired sensitivity to many ways of understanding the world. Sara Ahmed has written compellingly in "Against Students" about the sensitive student, indeed the so-called oversensitive student, who has been blamed for various assaults on higher education:

> The figure of the over-sensitive student is invested with power. The story goes: because students have become too sensitive, we cannot even talk about difficult issues in the classroom; because of their feelings we (critical academics) cannot address questions of power and violence, and so on. A typical example of this kind of rhetoric: "No one can rebut feelings, and so the only thing left to do is shut down the things that cause distress—no argument, no discussion, just hit the mute button and pretend eliminating discomfort is the same as effecting actual change." Or another:

"While keeping college-level discussions 'safe' may feel good to the hypersensitive, it's bad for them and for everyone else. People ought to go to college to sharpen their wits and broaden their field of vision." Here safety is about feeling good, or not feeling bad. We sense what is being feared: students will become warm with dull edges, not sharp enough in wit or wisdom. . . . Safe spaces are another technique for dealing with the consequences of histories that are not over (a response to a history that is not over is necessarily inadequate because that history is not over). The real purpose of these mechanisms is to enable conversations about difficult issues to happen. So often those conversations do not happen because the difficulties people wish to talk about end up being re-enacted within discussion spaces, which is how they are not talked about. . . . The very perception of some spaces as being *too soft* might even be related to the *harshness* of the worlds we are organizing to challenge.

I quote Ahmed at length here because this passage can help unravel several threads that together form the weave of liberal arts education—as well as some of its runs and frayed ends. I want to take some time working through these lines, as Ahmed's points move my own inquiry into liberal arts in useful directions.

First off, for Ahmed, the "oversensitive" student points to an imperative—and a skirting of this imperative—concerning "difficult issues" that should be broached and discussed in higher education contexts. Yet the so-called oversensitive student becomes a scapegoat for closing down the very sorts of difficult conversations that college *can* be a space for. Ahmed suggests that we reevaluate our rhetoric and treatment of this straw figure—indeed, that it is our obligation as professors to be sensitive ourselves, and with no upper limit to that sensitivity. This is especially true when dealing with matters of racism and sexism, matters hardly settled and indeed having been exacerbated in our age of post-truth, and with college now more than ever positioned to serve as a safe space for these issues to be taken seriously.

Where Ahmed ventriloquizes (in order to critique) the generic assertion, "People ought to go to college to sharpen their wits and broaden their field of vision," we might note a familiar specter of the liberal arts at work: the well-rounded individual who now is also given the extra assignment of sharpening their wits. And we should recognize this latter skill as "critical thinking" by another name. But it would seem that these two metaphorical actions are in tension, if not quite contradiction: *broadening* and *sharpening*. Ahmed picks up on this by locating a worry that oversensitive students who require safe spaces will end up with "dull edges" rather than sharp wits. But a well-rounded individual *should* have dull edges, geometrically speaking. The liberal arts ideal of the well-rounded individual and the vague demand for critical thinking are thus at odds.

Ahmed carefully defends the safe spaces of college as sites where learners can deal "with the consequences of histories that are not over" in a conscious, conscientious, *sensitive* fashion. This recalls how Frantz Fanon, in "The Lived Experience of a Black Man," frustratingly explains his dilemma as a black subject qua object in a white world. At one point, Fanon outlines a sort of ontological strategy as such: "If I were asked for a definition of myself, I would say that I am one who waits; I investigate my surroundings, I interpret everything in terms of what I discover, I become sensitive" (69). Such would seem to be an excellent rubric for liberal arts education. However, it also requires an acknowledgment of the harsh realities of the world (how "history hurts," to borrow a phrase from Fredric Jameson), as well as commitment to safe spaces—in ever permutating manifestations—in which earnest inquiry, intellectual development, *and* personal growth can take place.

Out of curiosity, I went back and looked at the mission statement of Hillsdale College. There are some terrifying parts of this statement (not surprisingly, as this school is known for its brazen politics), but for the purposes of concluding this particular chapter I want to focus on a seemingly innocuous section:

> The liberal arts are dedicated to stimulating students' intellectual curiosity, to encouraging the critical, well-disciplined mind, and to fostering personal growth through academic challenge. They are a window on the past and a gateway to the future.

Liberal arts are supposed to be a portal to the world, a window *and* a gateway: you *see* through it one way, and *go* through it another. This mixed metaphor may seem innocent enough, but it trembles on the fine point of the problem with liberal arts. People want college to be both practical (go forward) and theoretical (stop and wonder, reflect). Notice too how "students" move from a plural entity to the singular "well-disciplined mind." Here is another paradox: even at a bastion of individual freedom and self-governance such as Hillsdale College, the collective looms and cannot be so easily shaken off. Finally, there is the matter of "personal growth." This is a delicate thing, a soft and squishy vector, something that professors often do not want to be held accountable for. I have seen some colleagues recoil at the notion that we should teach our first-year students "life skills"—but since when is life *not* part of our purview?

This is an unfinished inquiry, necessarily incomplete. What I am advocating for is an ongoing calculation about what the liberal arts are doing rhetorically, functionally, and philosophically. How they help us clarify the projects of higher education, and when they obfuscate or mislead us. Far from being a simple or static model, we should understand the liberal arts to be complex, continually transmogrifying, and up for debate. If they are to be a safe space, this makes liberal arts hard to pin down—for good reason. Like Lydia Davis's awkwardly donned, itemizing signs on every individual, the liberal arts should be understood as capacious, indulgent, and fraught—but perhaps worthwhile if committed to, again and again, on ever changing grounds.

Sabbatical

As I've mentioned a few times already, I was on sabbatical as I put this book together. I opted to take the full year off from teaching, which my university grants me at two-thirds of my regular salary. Alternatively, I could have taken only one semester off and kept my full salary. But several of my senior colleagues encouraged me to take the entire year if I could make it work financially. When it comes to finishing research projects and really getting time to reflect on one's teaching, there is something to be said (so they said), for the full academic year plus two book-ending summers.

Sabbatical is not just about getting away from teaching. Like some other academics who have written about sabbatical, I actually missed being in the classroom. My students push me in dynamic and important ways—even when (especially when) it's uncomfortable. But it's all the other stuff on the campus that is gradually, cumulatively draining: Committee meetings. Drawn-out strategic planning sessions. Bombastic announcements of new administrative positions being created, followed by flat-toned assertions that there is insufficient funding for salary increases or tenure-track hires. Observing messy tenure-and-promotion cases drag out, and occasionally seeing mediocrity get rewarded. Yes, it was time for me to take a break, to regroup.

So Lara and I put our home up for rent on sabbaticalhomes.com to make up the other third of my salary, and we made plans for the coming year. That involved a temporary new school for Julien as well as countless logistical considerations. Then we headed up to Michigan, where we have family and where I planned to finish my book *Airportness* and then work on this one.

Over the summer and as the school year began, I found myself thinking a lot about this time: sabbatical. It's obviously an enormous privilege. And it seems downright sensible and humane when explained in a certain way: an extended time to rest and reflect on one's profession before returning to it, renewed and refreshed. I could feel that happening as the months went on. I was having new ideas about teaching, and I also had the time to do research and reading, which spurred fresh course ideas and suggested facets of my department's curriculum that might be honed.

One thing I noticed the year before was that my students had an awareness of what sabbatical was, and even what it *meant*. Toward the end of the year they would carp about not being able to take certain classes that I regularly teach this year; but then they were also curious about what I was going to be working on while I was away. I don't think I was imagining this: my students seemed to emanate a vague sense of pride in knowing that their professors could go on sabbatical and come back reinvigorated to teach after finishing big projects.

And really, consider what sort of message a sabbatical sends to students. The basic idea is that it is healthy and justifiable to give people time away from the grind. In fact, a sabbatical is a kind of direct acknowledgment that a career *is* a grind. This is not a message that career-planning services on campus probably want to convey. But such an acknowledgment is not necessarily a bad thing: some grinds are arguably worth sticking with—and being creative within—if then to discover deeper levels of satisfaction from one's work.

The underlying meaning of sabbatical is this: long-term jobs are *hard*, and people deserve real, significant breaks at consistent intervals. That is an important message that colleges and universities should want to communicate to students—especially institutions that want to train students to dedicate themselves to things, to make enduring commitments.

But then, sabbatical isn't fully a "break" at all. I had to apply for my sabbatical, referencing actual work in progress and articulating concrete goals. It is a break from teaching, yes—as well as from all the extra legwork of academic campus life. In truth, however, it is really choosing one type of academic work over another for a year.

This is a real benefit of sabbatical: I am able to focus solely on my writing this year. I spent the first six months finishing the one book and I delivered it to my publisher; and I spent the second half assembling and revising this book. I also have a book series that I coedit (Object Lessons), which involves innumerable daily tasks as well as regular correspondence with many authors and continuous, detailed tracking of manuscripts in progress. So I am working, for sure. In fact, my family might argue that I am working more than ever this year. But still: I am on sabbatical. It is a break from the grind, and I am very grateful for it.

It feels extravagant to write about this, to reflect on sabbatical itself, even though sabbatical *is* supposed to be a time for reflection. In the age of shrinking budgets and mass adjunctification, when so few college and university instructors have the opportunity to even apply for sabbatical, how dare I wax philosophical about this supreme luxury? Yet that is one of the very reasons I am writing about sabbatical in the first place: It's something we need to talk about, defend, and explain in terms of its importance.

As I watch institutions whittle away tenure-track positions, through voluntary severance packages and in favor of short-term, part-time, and ultimately disposable (or at least replaceable) faculty positions—positions that cost less and offer far fewer benefits—I realize that students are going to hear about sabbatical far less frequently, if at all. And likewise, scholars will cease to think about sabbatical as a goal, as a desired (and deserved) time to finish a big project or start a new one. (Of course, a certain amount of fantasy is at work here—it's not all hyperproductivity, all the time.) Perhaps worse, sabbatical can become a point of jealously and suggestive of a bifurcated faculty.

Unfortunately, rather than encouraging a culture of sabbaticals, campuses increasingly seem to be cultivating something quite different. This is the regime of constant work for plateaued if not decreased pay, ruthless competition among instructors and disciplines fighting for a piece of "the pie" (as I often hear my university's budget referred to), and reward structures than can appear ludicrously incommensurate across the institution. It can be almost comical to witness the sharp split between those on the campus wearing pressed suits and the disheveled professoriate. That split is a sign of a class division, and it also suggests a deeper divide: between the administration of finances and other operational matters, on the one hand, and education itself on the other. Not all upper administrators leave the classroom behind, of course; and there are certainly other class divisions around any campus. But my point here is that the divide between upper administration and permanent faculty can be particularly fraught.

Sabbatical is a privilege that everyone should defend and seek out, not something to be eliminated where it still exists. Many deans, provosts, and presidents probably enjoyed a sabbatical or two before they became full-time administrators. I hope they can recall the boon of those times and protect sabbaticals for their faculty.

One thing I didn't see coming in my sabbatical was the stress of the 2016 presidential election—especially the results. I've found myself thinking a lot about how I am going to teach differently when I return, given the very real sense that the country has taken a big step backward with respect to inclusivity and open-mindedness. My campus is home to one of the more diverse student bodies in the region, and so those are absolutely practical concerns. While I wasn't ready for such twists in my sabbatical year, I am trying to view them as further opportunities for reflection and critical writing, rather than as black holes of depression.

I have been extremely fortunate to be in a tenure-track position at a university that has supported my teaching and scholarship, and that has helped me to flourish even during tight periods. These are tricky times for higher education, with contradictory mandates to innovate while not risking positive outcomes. Assessment measures and strict syllabus guidelines rule the day, yet the incalculable magic of the classroom perseveres, delightfully impossible to pin down. This is the work of literature in our age of post-truth, again: to keep these dramas and tensions in mind as they play out on campuses, for all the competing narratives at play and forms of life at stake.

I hope that my sabbatical energizes me to return to the classroom with verve, and that my batteries get recharged for dealing with the grind of the job. More than those things, however: I hope that my junior colleagues will have this privilege to look forward to, as they set goals for their teaching and research. And I hope that my students continue to have sabbatical to ponder, far into the future.

Walking it off

Immediately after the presidential election in November 2016, the work of literature was the farthest thing from my mind. Or rather, I was overwhelmed by how lessons of power seemed not to have been learned, how dubious grand narratives were (again) shaping the course of the United States. But I felt powerless, even as it seemed like what I'd spent my adult life studying and teaching was more important than ever for working through this time. So I took walks, long walks.

*   *   *

The lakeshore before me is expansive: a ten-mile swoop of Lake Michigan coastline with no houses visible, only two public access points, and a backdrop of dense beech and maple forests that rise up from the pines and dunes below. I never get tired of this walk. In the distance, red foxes will dart down to the water and back to the cover of juniper before I get too close. Piping plovers and sandpipers dance at the water's edge, mining the wet sand for insect larvae. It is late in the season for dragonflies, but one iridescent-bodied outlier clings uncertainly to a blade of dune grass, likely its last flight before the wind shifts to the north tomorrow, and the first winter cold front pummels the peninsula.

The Sleeping Bear Dunes National Lakeshore is a stunning place, but I don't want to romanticize it too much. The nearby towns are reliant on a tourist economy, especially in the summer months—thus creating a familiar, vexed dynamic between the stoic locals and lavish vacationers. The place itself is beautiful, but can also be severe. Every year people die in the lake: from hypothermia after boating accidents, or from trying to swim in fierce rip currents. I've gotten lost here several times, in the labyrinthine cedar swamps and in the thickest parts of the forested hills in mid-summer, when the foliage blocks out the sunlight and disorients my sense of direction. The other day I ran across a mangled coyote carcass in a dogwood grove, apparently the result of some wild scuffle in the night. Like a crime scene, a foul scent lingered in the air and branches were bent and torn. Sometimes the lakeshore seems more like a Cormac McCarthy novel than an Emersonian treatise on Nature.

Now on the beach I notice another uncanny object: a dead loon washed up on the sand, its feathers crumpled by the waves and its head flipped back in an unnatural comportment. This isn't an anomaly—it's the fourth one I've seen today. The National Park has posted information to their website explaining that the recent die-off of loons along this lakeshore are caused by botulism E outbreaks, which they are studying. It's sad, as I've seen the loon population bloom here since I was a kid. When I was younger it was rare to see them on the inland waters, but now when I go out fishing, I will usually see a group of loons nearby, working a cove with their diving fishing techniques, or performing their mad splashing mating rituals while I wade the opposite shoreline. One summer evening Julien and I had been out in our canoe on a mirror-calm lake and we drifted to within twenty feet of three loons; when they made their haunting calls, from this close proximity the sounds had an altogether different sound than hearing them from afar, and Julien got a kick out of the expression "laughing loons."

*   *   *

During this time, I used these long walks as a kind of self-imposed therapy—physical sessions in which to cope with the aftermath of the recent presidential election, which completely blindsided me. I forced myself off the endless scrolling of my Twitter feed and the relentlessly depressing news cycle, and I just walked. Out on the lakeshore, I wondered about the last time Donald Trump was this far away from other people—if he has ever been. There's a kind of reflection made possible here that punctures the ego, and humbles one in the face of vast, enduring processes such as dune succession and cloud formation.

Human impact and pressures of course affect this place. The National Park Service dedicates a page on their website to climate change, encouraging visitors to take proper steps to decrease energy consumption and increase efficiency. The information also serves to reinforce a basic understanding: as impressive and sublime as this lakeshore is, it's not immutable. It's as fragile as it is precious. The dead loons on the beach are indicators of this fragility, stray white-dotted black feathers now mixed in with the snarls of dried dune grass and balloon strings.

Troublingly, the then president-elect's "policies" page on his website didn't even list the environment as a category. During the campaign, commentators noted the striking absence of the environment as a topic after each of the three presidential debates. It was like a case of widespread cultural amnesia, as if we had all forgotten that we actually live on a planet that is teetering on the brink of irreversible changes likely hastened by one species in particular: us. And now that Trump's reign is in full bloom, we see this denial playing out at the level of funding and support, not just for the National Parks, but for the wide range of environmental issues and ecological realities that riddle the country's conflicting desires for change.

I processed these thoughts as I walked the beach, at turns disheartened and inspired, confounded and calmed.

After the election my email inbox was relatively empty for days on end. I would normally have welcomed this aberration, except that it bespoke the mass shock and despair felt far and wide. At least, this seemed to be the case among the people with whom I was normally in contact: students, colleagues, and collaborators. Everyone was adjusting to this new reality that flies in the face of the causes and ideas that we have worked hard for everyday: gender equality, social justice, inclusivity, nondiscrimination, and environmental awareness, to name a few. There was a palpable sense among many that things had shifted for the worse. Hopefully in the long run we will counter all this by getting engaged, by taking action. But at that time we were still moving through the denial and anger stages.

I was fortunate to be at a remove as I contemplated these things. Up in Michigan we lived on a hillside in the northernmost edge of the national lakeshore, with only a few other houses in the vicinity. It gets dark in the afternoon, and the nights are long. On Election Day we had gone to bed early, happy to wait and see the results in the morning—we have no Internet or TV at home, and our so-called smartphones only work somewhat reliably if we hike to the top of the hill. We read to Julien and his little sister Camille, and tucked them in. We slept in blissful ignorance that night, and awoke to a nightmare. I tried to walk this nightmare off on the beach, day after day.

*   *   *

I still have a few miles to go before I get home. The white pine trees etch ideograms on the horizon, and stretches of wind-sculpted sand and mosaics of rocks mark my path. During this time I've found myself standing alone in the middle of this stretch of shoreline, no one in sight for five miles in either direction, at once comforted and in a heightened state of anxiety. Ecological thought and environmental activism seem more important than ever, and yet (or maybe *because*) at this exact time we are ushering in a leader who seems to have no regard for the very biosphere that surrounds the country he wishes to make great again.

The former camp counselor and river guide in me wishes I could wrest Donald Trump from his high tower, and take him on a long walk with me on this beach. I'd point out a thing or two, and let him be swept over by the expansiveness of this ecotone. But I know, too, that this is a simplistic and fraught desire: to let Nature be Trump's teacher. The truth is, Trump is himself a force of nature, a leader (for now) of an indicator species that is shaping the planet. The work of literature now is to trouble these categories between nature and culture like never before, to reveal how the narratives we weave make up the very fabric that we live in. How we tell our stories—and make them come true—is up to us.

I look up and see the contrails of a jet arcing in the sky, a wide-body airliner on its way somewhere, the engine condensation dissipating into the surrounding cirrus clouds. After the election I read several accounts by people who were on transatlantic flights as the polls closed and votes were tallied; they began their journeys in one world, and landed in quite another. I feel as though I had this experience, too, though on the ground and in a relatively remote and quiet place. Still, like the plane above me now, I sense that I am in motion, the planet continues its steady revolutions around our sun, and I won't stop working for what I believe in. One step back, two steps forward—that's what I've been telling myself of late.

Stepping along the shoreline, something crunches underfoot: it's a cluster of zebra mussels, an invasive species that infiltrated and changed the ecosystem of the Great Lakes over the past nearly thirty years. When I was a child zebra mussels first began appearing in huge quantities—sometimes there would be enormous drifts of their shells on the beach, altering the sand composition and making the lakeshore an alien space. The National Park Service and other agencies worked hard to curb the influx and keep the zebra mussels from spreading inland. It is an ongoing process, and a problem far from resolved. As zebra mussels are a filter feeder, they absorb toxins and have led to the spread of avian botulism. The zebra mussels, the loons, and myriad other creatures and vegetal beings are tangled up together on this coastline that, however beautiful it may appear from a certain vantage point, is anything from pristine.

Here I am seeing another complex facet of this place, and an allegory, perhaps, for this political moment. Whatever gains have been made over the previous eight years (or 50 years, or 150 years) things were far from perfect. A lot of work remains, and now that endemic hatred and structural inequalities seem to be amassing like so many zebra mussels on the shore, perhaps it will crystalize our determination to keep working, to attend to this world, amid all its complexities and mounting problems. Just as President Obama remarked that "history doesn't always move in a straight line" ("Obama Reckons with a Trump Presidency"), so too with ecology: it's a work in progress, and one that, if we're lucky, we can both respect *and* be an active part of, even as—especially when—invasions and disruptions occur. The beach is still here; the journey is far from over.

Trump in the anthropocene

When I teach my literature and environment class at Loyola, one of the first lessons I try to get across is a tricky one: "Nature" with a capital "N" is an artificial construct. This doesn't mean that there's no such thing *as* nature, but rather, that it's not something *over there*, detached from human life. Nature is, if anything, *everything*. Writing about nature—and reading across the history of nature writing—can bring this into sharp relief, as we see how different authors use rhetorical strategies and narrative and poetic devices to make nature appear more like Nature. So-called environmental writers are often very good at de-familiarizing the very stuff of life, if then to make readers pay attention and care for it all the more.

The day after the Women's March on Washington in January 2017, I took my children to the Smithsonian National Museum of Natural History. Amid the myriad exhibits I was struck by one piece of signage nestled into a wall within the aquatic life room. It was a sort of brief informative essay about the anthropocene. The sign diplomatically wondered whether or not this term should be used:

can we be so bold as to name an entire geological era after our arguably still young species? One way of answering this question is that we do it all the time, simply by rendering nature as something *other* than human in the first place. In other words, the Anthropocene has lurked as a cultural habit for a long time, before the word even emerged. It spilled out of smokestacks just as it infested nineteenth-century poems and essays named after "Nature."

It's one thing to consider the anthropocene when the incumbent political establishment acknowledges the significance of things like pollution, climate change, National Parks, environmental protections, and so on. In such an atmosphere, we can have spirited debates about the implications of the concept of the anthropocene, highlighting its different valences or offering alternative words. But this piece in the Smithsonian museum got me thinking: How are we to comprehend the anthropocene in an age of our new president, this demented leader who seems utterly unmoved by ecological thought? Does the term become another disparaged "big word" that loses all traction given a regime of swift deregulations and defunding of scientific and precautionary research? In short, now that we are seeing the swift rolling back of so many careful measures put in place over the past several decades, how are we to understand Trump in relation to the anthropocene?

I've been turning this over in my mind as I take my walks along the Sleeping Bear Dunes National Lakeshore, picking up beach trash. This stuff washes up on shore and accumulates, especially after a big storm. It's a mishmash usually consisting of balloon strings, plastic bottles, and bottle caps, and tiny fragments of larger plastic containers. It's a local snapshot of a global problem, one that we have come to know particularly well by the name "Great Pacific Garbage Patch"—that floating island in the Pacific Ocean the size of Texas, made of micro-plastics and other debris. These miniscule objects wreak havoc on certain bird species and other life forms, changing the planet demonstrably by threatening extinctions and upsetting the balances of ecosystems. Human waste has become such a vast thing, spread out across the globe, evident by traces and in glimpses but impossible to see as a totality—what Timothy Morton would call a "hyperobject." We're responsible for it, and yet it seems completely elusive and beyond our grasp.

Each day when I go back down to the beach, I fill another bag with these particulates of disposable fun, the detritus of so many summer vacations and freshwater boat rides. But how does Trump figure into this?

For one, we cannot dismiss him or his policies as *un*natural. Instead, as counter-intuitive as this may sound, we have to acknowledge Trump and his harmful policies as natural, and as symptomatic of where we have arrived as a species. From a certain angle it looks like suicide—as well as ecocide. But each of Trump's simplistic and grandiose orders so far has quickly exposed a teeming world of impassioned individuals and complex landscapes that can't be so easily contained or controlled. To borrow the words of eco-critic Stacy Alaimo, Trump may show us—if unpleasantly so—just how to "think the anthropocene subject as immersed and enmeshed in the world" (157). Trump, who can be seen as a sort of ambassador of the anthropocene, can also be understood as Alaimo's "anthropocene subject": he can't escape the realities of the world, and this all the more obvious as he tries to drown out the voices of others. In a perverse way, then, Trump could end up making the anthropocene a lot less controversial or debatable—he will make it chillingly visible as he continues to wade into quandaries that make his curiously ecological "swamp" metaphor appear more quaint than ever. In the offing of his presidency we see individuals and collectives newly rallying around causes that we may have assumed a few months ago were settled matters. It was never just about a fabulist wetland that could or should not be "drained"—again, what an odd idea—but rather it's a whole fragile, enmeshed planet with rising sea levels. And we're here for the duration.

So Trump might be reframed as nothing less than the perfect president to usher in more widespread awareness of the anthropocene at this moment. Someone who can single handedly (or strung along by his puppet masters) snarl global air travel, strand travelers, and cause thousands of protestors to rally at airports across the county. Someone who can bully the National Parks, only to spur outrage and clever social media pushback maneuvers. Someone who can so flagrantly ignore social and ecological currents as to, perhaps, incite entire new watersheds.

If the downside of the anthropocene is that we as a species have brought the planet to (or even beyond) the brink of mass species extinctions and widespread environmental collapse, the upside might be that we can acknowledge this and become, to use a buzzword, *proactive* and conscious participants in this epoch.

What would that look like? It wouldn't look like the ultra-wealthy pursuing habitation on other planets, or fortifying nuclear-proof bunkers in Kansas. It would involve slower processes such as community engagement, commitment to ecological education, and undoing our most wasteful and destructive habits. It would mean rethinking economic models and income gaps. It would mean trying, consciously and conscientiously, to bring about more balance rather than less, ecologically speaking. We have to work toward these things, even while knowing that there is no pure state of natural balance—flux is always the only game in town. We're not trying for perfect harmony—we're trying to survive, maybe even restore and better appreciate some of the biodiversity we have destroyed on our planet. And within these dynamic ecosystems, amid rampant threats and possible recoveries, how will we live out our time? What legacies will we leave, for our future generations and in the eventual fossil record, long after humans are gone?

These are serious questions that demand serious answers—not impulsive reactions or the frantic shoring up of resources. If we truly wish to treat human life with dignity, we cannot detach humanity from the whole planet, in all its intricacies and ongoing pulsations. The hubris of Trump might end up revealing the humility of humans living in—and *working with*—the anthropocene. It's an endless project—at least while we're here. But it's the project we cannot help but being a part of, whether we like it or not.

Another plane roars overhead as I finish this chapter, a high-powered screech just a few hundred feet above the trees. It's a private plane that I know well, a wealthy landowner in the county who flies up from Chicago each weekend to visit his lakeside Xanadu. By the time I get to the window there is no visual trace of the plane, just the muffled reverse thrust of the engines as the plane lands on the rustic runway nearby. The anthropocene is manifest in each private jet flight—and this cuts across people's personal politics, too.

Terminal democracy

"It must be very strange in an airplane, he thought" (25). This line is from Hemingway's *Old Man and the Sea*, and certainly we can imagine the aged fisherman gazing up into the night sky, watching the blinking lights of an aircraft as it passes above and pondering the vastly different comportments of those passengers as compared to the lowly angler's repose in his wooden skiff.

But it can be very strange in an airport, too.

On January 28, 2017, the news was flooded with images of stranded international travelers, crowded airport spaces, and frantic airline employees—all the result of Donald Trump's executive order imposing an immediate travel ban on visitors from seven nations in the Middle East. Travelers' stories were told, but ethnography seemed hapless in the face of Trump's cruel, sweeping order. By that evening protests were being held at airports around the country, at large airports and small. Even JFK's airport tram—that humble form of limited public transit—became a contested intermodal place after protesters were temporarily blocked from it. Collective action at or around airports could be seen all over social media, and soon enough, the hashtag #OCCUPYAIRPORTS was gathering momentum. Within days, a website dedicated to the airport protests popped up, offering state-by-state plans of action, resistance, and recourse in the event of arrests.

In these images of protest, the sterilized backdrops of airport architecture stood in stark contrast to the masses of protesters and their hastily scrawled signs. A prayer session occurred in the DFW baggage claim, urgently sanctifying what environmental psychologist Robert Sommer once called the "tight spaces" of airport waiting areas. Airport curbsides were no longer interstitial spaces but became effective staging grounds for highly visible demonstration. As Christopher Hawthorne argued in an article for the *Los Angeles Times,* "the airport is a hospitable host for protest precisely because of how *poorly* it works in terms of civic design on a typical day." This is true, but the traction of the protests wasn't just a matter of opportunistically seizing on the choke points in airport layouts. The ways in which airports *do* work as intended—how they manage to consistently sustain flow-through for millions of passengers every day, at times facilitating the movement of some at the expense of others—has also played a critical role.

History professor Jacob Remes pointed out on Twitter how airports are the perfect places for contemporary protests, "key sites of employment (often the biggest worksite in a city), surveillance, migration, and movement of goods and people." Not only that, the countless stories of racial profiling at security checkpoints and of passengers getting kicked off flights for speaking languages that others found suspiciously foreign suggests that racism and nationalism had long been acutely manifest in the routines of air travel.

Positioned at the nexus of so many different frontiers, physical and conceptual, airports seem to be foretold sites of vulnerability and inevitable chaos. They are linked to a long history of hijacking and terrorism, of course, and 9/11 propelled this aura further into the American cultural consciousness. Over the first decade of the twenty-first century, surveillance and identity checks have become ever more intense at US airports, indices of broader national and global tensions. Even those Americans accustomed to comfortable passage through whatever spaces they inhabit have felt airport misery in muted forms—not only during delays or cancellations but by the basic security clearance and boarding procedures that recast the traveling liberal subject as carefully tracked bio-cargo. Especially since 9/11, airport security checkpoints in the United States have seemed like minor police states, perhaps even to those inclined to trust the police.

After Trump's executive order tensions inherent to airports exploded to the fore, and two different kinds of chaos, each specific to a particular vulnerability, began to play out. The first of these had to do with the nature and extent of authority at airports. Behind the customs barriers and in waiting rooms, travelers were converted into suspects as airline employees and customs officials scrambled to make sense of (and ham-fistedly enforce) Trump's executive order. In these enclosed spaces, among some of these officials and their targets, it must have felt as though all the xenophobic pressures that had built up over the past fifteen years or so had broken through. Authorities with prejudices and personal axes to grind suddenly found themselves with the leeway to grind them unilaterally, exploiting the ambiguities and uncertainties around the executive order to discriminate, intimidate, detain, and block people at will—at least in the early hours of the ban.

This chaos was the murky underside of airport security: a toxic blend of ideological, logistical, and functional rule. Just beneath the ordinary procedures of airport security linger questions about who gets to be protected, who gets treated as threats, who gets to exercise arbitrary power, and who gets singled out for persecution. While global air travel seems to rest of on ideals of tolerance and fair treatment across disparate geographies and nations, these ideals are unevenly distributed at best. And Trump's executive order, beyond its practical snafus and blunders, exposed an underlying anti-democratic nature within air travel. Behind all the superficial order and worldly scope of modern flight, it turns out, are fractured dimensions of fear and hatred that can be exacerbated in an instant.

Later, as the protests began to mount, a second kind of chaos—a spatiotemporal chaos—took shape: crowds on the sidewalks, and clogging the terminal buildings, basically blocking the open spaces and flows of bodies that airports depend on. If airports are designed to facilitate temporary inhabitance and relatively rapid and constant transitions—what Damian O'Doherty has adeptly called "loungification"—the protests were able to use these design principles against themselves. As Hawthorne described it, "The narrow sidewalks; the pedestrian bridges leading to and from parking structures; the little islands of pavement where we wait for shuttle buses; the bi-level ring roads that encircle every airport: These were the stages on which the protests were most effective on their own terms, both in clogging traffic and producing media-ready images of an angry, loud and unnerved public." Yet this was no mere matter of poor design: It was always in airports' very nature to welcome, shepherd, and display such collective action—passengers routinely clump up and board together, linger around baggage carousels in masses, and cluster and fume together when there's a hiccup in the system. The protests were like a major wave of airline delays or cancellations, but instead of domestic flights in question, people were responding to entire ontological trajectories suddenly put on hold.

It's no wonder that protesters were so deft at mobilizing and occupying public airport zones. Travelers on private jets, like Trump, have an experience that is utterly incommensurate with the routines of commercial air travel. Whereas Trump disingenuously lashed out at US airports as being like "third world countries" in the first presidential debate—yet how many hours had he himself ever spent in these places of dead time, indignity, and rote work?—ordinary American travelers have internalized the spaces and procedural logics of air travel, and could put that knowledge to use in a readily legible public expression of resistance. This was an act of the work of literature in an age of post-truth, using the semiotic frameworks and interpretive structures against themselves: Security was built-in (Transportation Security Administration agents aplenty); amphitheater-like areas were easily improvised; a continually renewed public audience passed by; the routes to the sites of protest were well established: These familiar aspects are all part of what I have called "airportness": the ways that ordinary travelers internalize—and come to naturalize—the patterns and textures of commercial air travel.

Of course, not all travelers experience these patterns and textures in the same way. Earlier that same week, before the ban was signed, something else happened at JFK: a fifty-seven-year-old Massachusetts man was charged with hate crimes after harassing and kicking a Delta employee who was wearing a head scarf, saying, among other things, "Trump is here now. . . . He'll get rid of all of you." This incident occurred not in the open spaces of the airport concourses, or in the sorts of places where the protests would occur a few days later—but in the Delta Sky Club lounge.

What Trump seems to despise about airports is precisely what makes them airports: the tenuous messes, the congestion, the high visibility, and the people there. His rhetoric describing US airports as "third world" raised their profile as sites of crisis, places where some supposed form of un-Americanness could already be seen plainly. But the nature of what is "unacceptable" remains open to contest, and the shared indignities and hopeful fantasies that airports structure for ordinary, non-elite travelers provides an entirely different basis for determining that and expressing it. Little did Trump realize that in directing further attention to airports, he was loading a weapon that would not be entirely his to wield.

Airports were already fraught borderlands where disconcerting, seemingly arbitrary regimes of identity checks and detentions get carried out, where the class privilege to avoid much of the procedural despair can literally and explicitly be bought. But after the travel ban, the airport's abject zones—customs lines, waiting rooms, blazingly lit hallways leading to secret interiors—became public spectacles anew, where it wasn't inconvenience and inefficiency on display but something like the rapid degeneration of democracy. And alongside it, something hopeful was happening: people were discovering that airports were primed for swarming by the resistance.

What goes on at airports never stays at airports. What occurs in these nodes ripples outward, affecting distant geographies, logistics, and emotions. They become texts, open to reading—and revisionary practices.

On Apple News, a *Washington Post* article "How the World Is Responding to Trump's Travel Ban" was given a cover illustration of a stylized route map, similar to the sort you find in the back of an in-flight magazine. The airports were glowing blue dots, with the lines of flight paths gracefully arcing up and over a slightly tilted earth. A common enough image, it was nonetheless an odd one to use given the context. Once a diagrammatic expression of the hope of cosmopolitanism and a wide-open world woven together by flight, it has taken on new meaning in the context of the ban and the protests. It now suggests not safe points of origin and destination but contested sites of capture, deportation, and resistance. These are no longer curvatures of connection, but stark lines of division and discrimination. It now resembles something more like a battle map for the Trump regime, or a chart highlighting the epidemiological spread of what it regards as unwanted elements, vectors of transmission that demand containment.

Airports, in Marc Augé's oft-cited term, are "non-places": in-between zones that facilitate the various modalities and circulation cycles out of which contemporary life is comprised. If the airport is a non-place, it is now the site where Trump's administration is trying to turn people into non-persons. With Trump's travel ban we are seeing how such generic sites, supposedly devoted to *any* traveling subject, can be used to heat up and vent simmering forms of nationalism: airports can be turned against *specific* traveling subjects, at will. However, this generic quality also allows airports to be occupied, to become sites of resistance. Any airport stands as a ready-made point of protest. This double-sided feature of airports is itself rising in temperature. As much as Trump and his ilk can use airports to sort and intimidate people, others have discovered that airports are useful flashpoints in terms of their sensitized public status.

Trump's clampdown on international airports is less about the experience of air travel itself than a symbolic rejection of cosmopolitanism and tolerance. But it is also much more than a symbolic gesture. Or rather, Trump's travel ban symbolizes much more than its supposed limited and temporary scope. It does not involve just the few countries named and the travelers following these routes, and it doesn't merely involve international airports. The executive order appears to have been rolled out by design in a confusing and disruptive fashion, allowing no time for airlines or government officials to prepare for its implementation. This has had significant financial implications for the airlines, who were forced to adjust to the executive mandate at their expense (at the very least in terms of time, reputation, and so on). And it placed officials in the position of having to deploy state power with no clear sense of the legality of doing so, as court orders were issued and variously defied.

Disrupting both state and airline protocols without warning, and instigating an enormous waste of time, money, and resources would seem to run counter to Trump's expressed wish to make airports great again. But in fact, this action sheds far more disturbing light on what his regime takes to be "greatness": extreme vetting, deepening strains of insecurity, and ever more paranoia. The executive order was a naked demonstration of the current regime's willingness and intent to suspend the rights and protections afforded by the Constitution on the basis of religion, nationality, or ultimately any other arbitrary marker of identity, even at the cost of vast economic inefficiencies or the disempowering of the judicial branch.

Even as Trump's order was scaled back, curbed, and revised, the damage was done: Trump revealed himself to be president of a terminal democracy. As liberal democracy teeters or, perhaps, reaches its unfortunate apotheosis, airports have become places to be watched not only for the emergence of nationalist politics but also for collective acts of resistance. Airports have never been neat and tidy border spaces. Now more than ever we may see these sites as vulnerable not just in terms of who can enter and leave, but also who can occupy them. Terminals can be places where the universality of certain human rights can be championed and defended, and not merely a place where such ideas are terminated.

This book was not supposed to be about airports, but they have become newly interpretive sites in the age of post-truth. Airports are a topic I continue to return to, in day-to-day life as well as in my writing and literature classrooms. If the work of literature is somehow about place, it is equally about non-place and about refusing to simply pass by or through such sites unaware.

Hunting for morels, finding a mess

Far from any airport, I'm walking through an aspen grove next to a steep ridge, looking up at the mossy bases of big ash trees. They have a shaggy, mottled look—evidence of the emerald ash borer beetles that have ravaged them over the past decade. Still not able to focus on novels or much else besides a stray poem or story here and there, I spend much of my time outside.

Morel mushrooms grow near these trees, and they seem sparser with each year that passes, as dead ashes crisscross the forest floors. The white morels (which tend to look more gray or even yellow, depending on where you find them) are often thought to appear toward the end of the season. First, the elusive black morels appear. But everyone's noticed a dearth of black morels this year. Some people say it's just cyclical, or that the mushrooms will adjust and find another sort of tree to live with. But I sense something else going on, something to do with our age of post-truth.

I remember valleys carpeted with black morels when I was young. The black morels were often petite, but always intricately sculptural and beautiful, gnomic and nestled between Jack in the Pulpit and Trillium flowers. This year I found only five, in a gravelly patch that I recalled only moments before stumbling upon it, deep in the woods. Finding morels often works like this for me: I head out of the house with a vague sense of direction, but usually I don't clue in to the exact spot I'm headed to until just before I'm on top of it. Then there is a flash of deep recollection or attunement, and I look down and there they are.

It's early June as I write this; the season is effectively over. There are still a few morels to be found, but by this point they will most likely be slug-nibbled and sun burned, way past their prime. While I heard a few rumors about big hauls of morels discovered in swampy areas, most people I talked to were left flummoxed by this year's crop. People often tell stories about how these mushrooms are mysterious; morels will hide and then show up almost whimsically in abundance, right before your eyes. Case in point: a couple weeks ago I went on a two-hour walk looking for morels, ranging over some fairly remote areas of the national lakeshore that should have been bursting with mushrooms. But I didn't find a single one. The following morning I walked out of my front door to see a plump, fresh white morel popping out from between two rocks a foot away from the house—as if winking at me. And as Anna Lowenhaupt Tsing writes in *The Mushroom at the End of the World*, "When gathering mushrooms, one is not enough; finding the first encourages me to find more" (288). Even after a fruitless hunt the day before, I am suddenly motivated to try again.

It's especially fun to teach kids to hunt for morels. Children are literally closer to the ground, and once they learn to spot morels they can be astonishingly adept at picking them out of the dizzying patterns of leaves and ground cover. Julien and Camille are both adept mushroom hunters, and at peak season I can barely keep up with them as they dash through the forest finding clusters of morels beneath leaves and by tree trunks.

This year's black morel scarcity invariably comes up when I'm talking to locals about how many they've found so far (but never *where*—morel hunters are notoriously cagey about their secret spots). One thing that hasn't come up is the C word—or, rather, the CC words: *climate change*. No one has ventured that climate change might have something to do with the disappearance of the black morels. And to be clear, I'm not at all sure that myself. Still, it is surprising that I haven't heard the phrase uttered by the people I've talked to who are saddened by the low turnout in what, by most accounts, was supposed to be a good spring for morels (cool, plenty of ground moisture, etc.).

Then again, "climate change" carries so much rhetorical baggage—and particularly right now. To cite climate change as the probable cause of *any* ecological shift or perceived imbalance is to come out strongly, if indirectly, against the Trump administration and its ilk. They are fighting words, politically speaking. Furthermore, to evoke "climate change" with sincerity is to admit some kind of vulnerability, and to cast some blame at humans—at *ourselves*. We are complicit. The way climate change is understood and wielded, is a necessarily self-critical concept, and self-criticism is hardly practiced by leaders and followers who recite mantras of pride, nationalism, and winning at any cost. Climate change is for losers.

But then, we're definitely losing a lot of trees back in the woods, and mushrooms too. Even if there's not a direct causal relation here, there are certain realities that are uncomfortable to acknowledge, but impossible to ignore: irregular weather patterns, freakily massive storms, some species going extinct, and other species disseminating wildly. *Climate change* has become a euphemism for a whole host of difficulties involving ecological dynamism and evolutionary impermanence: it's about admitting that we will never be "winners"—also that life is not a war, and not a game. To take climate change seriously is to signal a willingness to roll up one's sleeves and commit to various real-world problems, and actions: reducing waste, minimizing one's footprint, caring for other species, and so on. So much simpler to keep our heads down, our mouths shut, looking for these ineffable, tasty mushrooms.

One of the deep ironies of morels is how they thrive in disturbed landscapes. A mountainside ravaged by wildfire, black stumps spread out like some motley cemetery? Perfect for morels the following spring. A hillside logged, left stripped and ragged? Morels will move right in. A rutted out road riddled with rocks and unapologetic tire tracks? There they are! So even if climate change were to have something to do with the vanishing black morels, who's to say that they wouldn't spring up just after the closure of the anthropocene? Morels may remind us about our temporary spell on this planet, and they may also teach us to seriously ponder the messier aspects of coexistence.

Cormac McCarthy's *The Road* brings morels to life on the page in exactly this way, as tenacious organisms in a wasted landscape:

> He stopped. Something in the mulch and ash. He stooped and cleared it away. A small colony of them, shrunken, dried and wrinkled. He picked one and held it up and sniffed it. He bit a piece from the edge and chewed.
> What is it, Papa?
> Morels. It's morels.
> What's morels?
> They're a kind of mushroom.
> Can you eat them?
> Yes. Take a bite.
> Are they good?
> Take a bite.
> The boy smelled the mushroom and bit into it and stood chewing. He looked at his father. These are pretty good, he said.
> The pulled the morels from the ground, small alien-looking things he piled in the hood of the boy's parka. (40)

This is one of the infrequent scenes of gustatory pleasure and treasure finding in *The Road*, and it hints duly at the impoverished ecosystem and yet at the persistence of certain life-forms. It's a strongly ambivalent moment in the novel, reflecting ecological knowledge reflected and passed on—but also hinting at the strange otherness of the fungus, as well as their utter scarcity. They are "good" but this goodness is set against a backdrop—indeed, a whole encompassing landscape—of horror and desolation.

In Emily St. John Mandel's *Station Eleven* (which I have begun teaching instead of *The Road* in my Twentieth-Century American Fiction course) there are no morels to speak of, although much of the novel takes place in prime mushroom country—up in Michigan. But there are other scavenged provisions that appear in this novel, and they are stored in an interestingly other postapocalyptic site:

> there were still airplanes here and there. They stood dormant on runways and in hangars. They collected snow on their wings. In the cold months, they were ideal for food storage. In summer the ones near orchards were filled with trays of fruit that dehydrated in the heat. (31)

Station Eleven reminds us that the messier aspects of coexistence involve other weird remainders of the anthropocene as well: the airfields around which mushrooms and fruit might continue to grow, long after the planes have been grounded for good.

Flying through nowhere

Driving up to the Cherry Capital airport in Traverse City, Michigan, the first thing you see is an artificial waterfall pouring over a concrete slab. It might remind you of something you've seen elsewhere. Yes, that's it: it resembles the Frank Lloyd Wright masterpiece "Fallingwater," the house with a river running artfully through it, and where Brad Pitt and Angelina Jolie, in better times, celebrated Pitt's forty-third birthday.

Approaching the curb and then setting foot into the actual terminal in Traverse City, you may notice more stylistic nods to the famous twentieth-century American architect: familiarly cantilevered rooflines, rectilinear stained glass patterns, and flower pots in the baggage area that are actual copies of Wright originals, replete with his iconic signature. My grandfather, who was himself a proud owner of a Frank Lloyd Wright home, once told me in passing that Wright never had any interest in designing airports. That bit of apocrypha notwithstanding, the Traverse City airport utilizes an amalgam of Wright allusions—even an access road called "Wright Drive"—to signal regional value, and a sense of uniqueness. These accouterments say *here you are in the Midwest, where things like this happen.* (Never mind that there are no Frank Lloyd Wright houses in Traverse City, per se.)

Over the past seventeen years I have spent a lot of time thinking about how airports achieve senses of place, and how they reflect and mesh with nearby city centers or farther flung destination points. Questions of this sort came up during a radio program I was part of, concerning the Kansas City airport and a heated debate among locals there about whether the existing terminal should be preserved or renovated, or whether it should be demolished and cleared for a new, "world class" structure ("Airports and KCI"). The lines of debate tended to fold back onto what the city itself stood for, and how people felt differently about Kansas City's status and place in the broader country, and even the world. Some listeners called into the show and praised the old terminal's convenience and architectural significance, suggesting that it was special to them, and that Kansas City shouldn't have to try to be better than it already was. Others complained about the terminal's dated qualities and insisted that the airport was holding Kansas City back from taking its place on the national stage as a bourgeoning locus of growth and connection.

What struck me by the conclusion of the show was the variety of viewpoints about what the airport meant to the people of Kansas City, and how these competing meanings depended on divergent senses of place and the narratives these senses upheld. In other words, it was a case for the work of literature. The airport represented a symbolic gesture announcing the Kansas City's self-regard, and was expected to transmit the city's importance outward. For some, a sparkling new terminal would make travelers take the city seriously (and always implicitly at the expense of *other* Midwestern cities and *their* shabby airports). For others, the existing terminal—even with its retrograde designs and hindrances—was a matter of pride: it said that Kansas City was good enough as is, and wouldn't be cowed by any juggernaut imperative to upgrade its travel facilities like every other scrambling mid-size city in the country. What both sides missed, it seemed to me, was the basic reality of air travel as an integrated network, as well as the delicate matter of airports having to be simultaneously generic *and* uniquely place-based. Every airport has to deal with this enigma, balancing its distinctive qualities with the need to be forgettable, a mere node leading to somewhere else.

Another dilemma has to do with the tension between the place itself and the airport, which is frequently many miles from one's actual destination. Airports are often not technically "in" the cities or towns whose names they bear. Several people on the radio show noted that the Kansas City airport was a good twenty-minute drive from downtown, and that it therefore privileged certain types of potential fliers who had means to other forms of mobility. Another example: the airport I used to work at is called the Bozeman Yellowstone airport, but it is not in Bozeman (it's in Belgrade, eight miles to the northwest), and Yellowstone National Park is a solid hour and a half away (when there's no snow). Still, airports are expected to reference their place-names, sometimes with local fare and other times through imagery or art—such as large format photographs of local buildings or skylines, or pictures of spraying geysers or sculptures of bears and geese. But this stuff can come across as perfunctory or even as campy, degrading the place rather than doing it justice. Everyone knows, after all, that you're just in the airport at this point: you're not *really* there yet.

But then why should people expect a new, fancy terminal to deliver some greater sense of significance or meaning? The technologies will be outmoded almost as soon as they are installed, and that travel conditions are constantly shifting depending on weather, mechanical issues, geopolitics, and myriad other factors. People ought to recognize that an airport will always be just that: an airport, fraught with contingencies and uncontrollable variables. Still, people seem to want *more* from airports—and they want *their* airports to be special, better than the rest somehow. Make *my* airport great again!

Herein lies another problem. Airports, just like towns, cities, and even countries, can never exist in isolation from one another. And to pit cities—and their airports—as competing actors on some sort of stage is to forget or to ignore a fundamental aspect of place: it's the fact of being connected, and *inter*connected. Being (or wanting to become) the best place is certainly fashionable in some quarters, but this always results in ill-fated, rabid competition—for to be the best necessitates someone (or somewhere) else being the *worst*, and a vicious cycle inevitably ensues.

In spite of desires and attempts to stand out and be the best, airports almost cannot help but be universally bland, sunk in an ether of standardization and banality. And a lot this fate has to do with the more dispersed, individually felt experiences of jet lag and general stress, as passengers shuffle through concourses in a fog or under duress. Over the years I've track these sorts of things in literature, as a way to account for the complex feelings people have for airports. Consider this scene in the recently published short story in the *New Yorker*, "It's a Summer Day," by Andrew Sean Greer:

> He floats through the Frankfurt Airport in a dream, thinking, Passport, wallet, phone, passport, wallet, phone. On a great blue screen he finds that his flight to Turin has changed terminals. Why, he wonders, are there no clocks in airports? He passes through miles of leather handbags and perfumes and whiskeys, miles of beautiful German and Turkish retail maids, and, in this dream, he is talking to them about colognes, and letting them giggle and spritz him with scents of leather and musk; he is looking through wallets, and fingering one made of ostrich leather; he is standing at the counter of a V.I.P. lounge and talking to the receptionist, a lady with sea-urchin hair, about his childhood in Delaware, charming his way into the lounge, where businessmen of all nationalities are wearing the same suit; he sits in a cream leather chair, drinks champagne, eats oysters; and there the dream fades.

To put this scene in context, the "dream" here is a sleeping pill induced haze experienced by the main character during a connection between flights. But even through this blurred perspective the details of the airport couldn't be more crystalline. The main character observes the eerie temporality of terminals ("no clocks"), blue screens announcing seemingly inevitable gate changes, a profusion of consumer goods, intimate yet corporate exchanges with "beautiful" if interchangeable customer service representatives. All architecture and design nuances are distilled into the non-place, and any semblance of locality is elided by the miasma of routine transfer. While a mere passing scene in a longer story about our character's trip far beyond the Frankfurt Airport, this terminal walk contaminates the rest of the story, exposing the fuzzy promises of individual mobility at its apex. While the airport effectively delivers this passenger through his almost disembodied dream state, it also stands as a haunting, monolithic structure that could be anywhere, doing this same thing to anyone—anyone with enough privilege and status, that is.

What would a democracy of airports look like? Is there a way to embrace and build airports that would honor places without needing to elevate them above others? How might airports display senses of place without eliding the complexities of living in space, with and among others, on myriad scales? It is well known that air travel has become much more affordable and accessible to a wider range of people, over the past fifty years or so; but for whom does air travel remain out of reach, and what places are still cut off from or contaminated by the modern miracle of flight? And why does air travel feel like flying through nowhere, much of the time?

I am working on this chapter at 3:43 in the morning when I become aware of a distant rumble of jet engines overhead. I toggle over to an Internet browser window and consult Flight Aware, searching the sky above me via air traffic satellite information to find out what I'm hearing. It's a Boeing 767, operated by Cargojet and en route from Calgary to Hamilton, Ontario. Here is another part of airport life that people tend to forget about: the intricate, ongoing networks of cargo transport that interweave and make our consumer culture possible, for better and for worse. For these flights, terminal design matters far less than runway layouts, proximity to vast warehouses and ground shipping facilities, and refueling stations. Seen from this perspective, humans are merely another form of the multitudinous objects transferred from site to site, from place to place, biocargo shipped around this planet that is our temporary home.

When we think about airport design and senses of place, it's worth contemplating the bigger place that connects us all. How might new terminals reflect *this* place, in addition to our smaller (if no less important) places we call origin, connection, or destination?

Stuck

I can't quite let go of that radio program about the Kansas City airport. As I mentioned above, the locals debated whether to preserve and renovate the existing structure, or whether to demolish the old terminal in order to build an entirely new, "world class" terminal. The back and forth ranged from nostalgia for the golden age of flight and sentiments of "it's good enough for us" about the iconic airport, to strong desires for Kansas City to flex its muscles and join other US cities on the world stage. By the end of the program there was no clear single direction or unified feeling about the status of the airport, and what should happen next. If anything, I detected strong disagreement and confusion about what construction at the Kansas City airport should look like, and for what reasons.

One point that I had tried to make during the discussion was that any attempts to redesign or build anew had to take into consideration twin demands that are in tension: for an airport to be memorable and distinctive, it must have unique elements and local flavor; but at the same time, the airport must be someplace you want to leave, to get to the *actual* destination (like a nearby city or farther flung site, like a national park). While this is something of a paradox, it is not altogether impossible: some airports do manage to harness a geographically specific feeling while remaining generic enough to keep travelers moving. The trick is always how to achieve this balance of opposing forces.

Something that nagged at me after the discussion was a series of tweets by one listener, which included this observation:

> It doesn't matter where you are, if you're "stuck" you're going to hate it.
>
> @KatieKMCO

Even though the context of this comment was airport delays specifically, the sentiment struck me as having serious ecological implications. How much scientific knowledge has been gained from patient observation—from lingering in what for some time may have felt like being merely "stuck"? Biological processes do not always happen quickly, or at the speed of human will or immediate perception. Take more pedestrian examples, such as bird watching, insect identification, or foraging: isn't part any naturalist's pleasure in fact derived from *waiting* for the unknown, and sometimes feeling stuck in the process? People don't have to hate being stuck—it might be more accurately reevaluated as part of the experience, and a key part at that.

Allow me a brief digression: not too long after this radio show, I was fly fishing along the shoreline of a favorite lake in the Sleeping Bear Dunes National Lakeshore, a small body of water that I've fished since I was a kid and a place that I know quite well. The morning had started out clear, but within an hour moody clouds were forming over the hills, rolling off the Lake Michigan coast. This happens from time to time in the microclimate of the peninsula I live on: sudden strong storms form too fast for radar to pick up, caused in part (as I understand it) by the temperature differential when the air over the lake slams into the air rising up from the landforms at the shoreline, the steep dunes and the dense beech and maple forests. Soon thunder boomed, and the sky grew dark. I heard the rain on the trees across the lake, and half a minute later the storm was upon me, pounding rain and lightning cracking overhead. I had been dropped off that morning and had no way to get home or to a car quickly, so I took shelter beneath a white pine at the edge of the water, crouching beneath the branches and watching the lake surface get whipped into a froth. I put my fly rod under a nearby dogwood, so as not to attract an errant bolt of lightning. I had no way of knowing how long the storm would last and so I just sat there, waiting it out. I wasn't doing what I had planned to do that morning, I wasn't fishing. The passing minutes became indeterminate. I was stuck. And it was great! I relished the smells that rose up from the freshly soaked ground, the shapes of the swarthy clouds undulating over the hills, and the sheets of rain marching across the lake. I had to change my perspective, to focus on something I had not anticipated—and by doing so, I enjoyed what was out of my control, what I hadn't planned on.

My point is this: in so called nature we do this all the time. We greet the unexpected, and understand that it is part of the experience of being alive, part of being in the wild. So how is it that airport spaces deactivate this capacity, or seem to render it obsolete? Why can't people experience *stuckness* in the airport similarly to how it is treated in the great outdoors? (Or, for that matter, in literature!) Being stuck—temporarily, of course—is a way of getting entangled in ecological vines. Life always goes on, even when time seems like it's standing still. And this is where airports come in.

Airports have an odd relationship with ecological thought, and I don't mean this in a purely philosophical way. Airports can be some of the wilder places people move through: see weather delays; see bird strikes; see air rage. But in these strange ecotones nature wears the mask of culture.

When I consulted the Kansas City International Airport Terminal Area Master Plan—a 594-page document guiding the new development, at least in theory—I found that the word "ecology" shows up *not once*. It's the same for "ecological." The word "environment" fares better, appearing on fifty pages of the plan. But "environment" is a squirmy thing in the context of airport planning: at times it means the physical space encompassing the airport; at other times it denotes wildlife species, plants, and water systems on site (or passing through); and at still other times it stands for "Historic, Architectural, Archaeological, and Cultural Resources" (2–44). The environment seems conspicuously to be an *obstacle* for airport construction, something to be avoided or mitigated as design and building take place.

Seeking answers, or at least more questions, I emailed a Kansas City environmental education organization called Bridging the Gap, which is dedicated to "connecting Environment, Economy, and Community." I inquired whether there were any issues of local concern regarding the airport site and the surrounding ecosystem, or other environmental considerations. I was especially curious if there are certain key species or sensitive populations that might be under the spotlight, what with the new airport plans. Executive Director Kristin Riott replied promptly with a blunt assessment: "I would think any species negatively impacted by the flight paths of planes would have either been killed or relocated long ago." This implied a dismal truth: airports take up so much physical space, interrupting migration paths and watersheds, that to approach them several decades later from an environmental standpoint is to immediately confront so much that has likely already been lost. I was reminded of Hannah Palmer's moving book *Flight Path*, which investigates the demolished and largely forgotten neighborhoods beneath Atlanta's sprawling airspace, where Palmer grew up: humans are not exempt from an airport's ability to devastate biospheres.

But then in her email to me, Riott went on to wonder:

Perhaps your questions could be turned around: What can we do to protect and restore local wildlife while we're building the new airport? What are the opportunities to improve its environmental impacts vs. the old one? (By, for example, capturing storm water runoff, planting heavily so that trees and other vegetation can improve air quality, etc.)

These ideas intrigued me, and struck me as worthy of serious consideration. What *would* it mean for an airport design to really take the local ecosystems, flora, and fauna seriously as co-participants in the complex life world of this transit space? Would such sensitized attunement grind airport construction—not to mention flight in general—to a halt? Or might such planning be able to improve the ways that the airport is built and inhabited for years to come?

Indeed, another section of the master plan lists a variety of various other airport sustainability initiatives, ostensibly as models for new construction at the Kansas City airfield. Yet these initiatives end up reading like an obligatory, grudgingly assembled laundry list: LEED certification; preferential parking for alternative fuel vehicles; carbon footprint reduction; use of recycled materials in building; natural lighting, and so forth. All these things are obviously fine and well-intentioned, but they still serve to make the environmental impact of the airport seem like a piecemeal matter of peripheral compromises and symbolic gestures, rather than a permeating and conditioning fact of existence—something inescapable, something we're stuck with. Something we might appreciate being stuck with: our environment, that is.

Reading through a chapter of the Master Plan called "Environmental Overview/Baseline," I focus on a Pros/Cons section that delineates the differences between building on several distinct sites on the airport property, including where the existing airport sits. One phrase appears three times: "Site is previously disturbed." Twice this is cited as a Pro (less new ground to pave), and once it is a Con (more old contaminated materials to deal with), but the idea lingers in my mind. We're stuck with a site that is previously disturbed. This is the acknowledgment that the space of the airport has always already impacted the surrounding ecosystem, and new construction will inevitably have to deal with matters of pollution, toxic cleanup, and sensitive life-forms that exist in tandem with the bustling, loud, and terraforming complex.

On a larger scale, we're stuck with airports for the time being. Flight is a preferred mode of transit, for good and for ill. But given this reality, what would it look like for an airport building project to truly prioritize the local environment, to lessen rather than increase the impact on other species of life? What if the new Kansas City airport not only avoided the tendency of terminals to slip into non-place, but also became a leading example of building for the future—not just the future of aviation, but of sustainable coexistence on a larger scale? What kind of narratives would be generated by such development, and where would they travel? These questions might seem grandiose in their scope. Kansas City seems in many ways doomed to recreate the same old airport problems, even if some locals continue to raise questions concerning the project's environmental impact. Nevertheless, now—precisely because of our precarious times—is when airports might be seriously reassessed, and if not abandoned altogether, then perhaps reimagined so as to nestle more harmoniously within the planet's vast, intricate networks of travel and life. Kansas City airport, while now stuck as a site previously disturbed, may yet become a test case for how human aviation impacts might be lessened, possibly even reversed.

Tick thinking

Lydia Davis's tiny stories are infested with duly tiny insects. They collaborate with her, and they show up as refugees and companions. In one story, an out-of-place caterpillar concerns her and distracts her from her daily tasks; in another story, a fly darts across her paper as she writes. Bugs *bug* Davis, in weirdly productive ways.

Over this sabbatical I've had my own insect assistants—especially ticks. But be warned, these probably aren't the musings about ticks that you want to read. Popular takes on ticks cast them as sinister enemies of our species, and offer tips and advice for evading them, extracting them, and killing them. As a recent *Slate* article called "The Year of the Tick" put it, "let's all wage war." Against ticks, that is. The article advises after removing a tick from the skin, "then saving the tick in a sealed plastic bag so that you can later identify and potentially test it. It'll dry out and die in there, too. I rather enjoy watching ticks perish."

The *Slate* author's attitude may seem like common sense and easily justifiable, from a human-centric point of view—which some people would argue is all we can ever have, as humans. But there may be good reasons to reassess this perspective, to step back from such strong rhetoric that condones ready violence against ticks. For, as Stacy Alaimo explains in her book *Exposed*, "The anthropocene suggests that agency must be rethought in terms of interconnected entanglements rather than unilateral 'authoring' of actions" (156). We don't have to completely agree on the definition of the anthropocene (or even what to call this era we're in) to recognize it at work in the *Slate* article, where the author confidently situates humans as having a deciding role in the fate of ticks—at least in relation to humans and human communities. That is anthropocentric *thinking* and "authoring," whether or not one believes in the Anthropocene per se, or not.

Compare the sentiments of the *Slate* article with philosopher Giorgio Agamben's meditation on a tick's *Umwelt* in *The Open*: "Let us try to imagine the tick suspended in her bush on a nice summer day, immersed in the sunlight and surrounded on all sides by the colors and smells of wildflowers, by the buzzing of the bees and other insects, by the birds' singing" (46). Bracket the larger questions that occupy the book, and the fact that the tick's phenomenology is complicated by Agamben's following paragraphs; it is nevertheless an imaginative leap, and a compassionate hesitation, that resides in the invitation to consider the tick on its own terms, entangled in a many-layered, variegated environment.

Or consider biologist David George Haskell's own encounters with a tick, in *The Forest Unseen*:

A tick perches at the tip of a viburnum branch, a few inches from my knee. I suppress the urge to flick the pest away. Instead, I lean in to see the tick for its own sake, trying to look beyond my quick mental dismissal of it as a mere pest. The tick senses my approach and lifts the front four of its eight legs in a frenzied wave, grasping at the air. (117)

Again, here we see a markedly different approach to tick thinking, an attempt at cohabitation—however fleeting. The biologist pauses with the tick, and learns from it. Haskell's meditative sojourn with the tick is not entirely romantic, and concludes with an acknowledgment that "Fear of ticks is etched in my nervous system by the experience of many, many lifetimes. Our battle with questing ticks is at least sixty thousand times older than the Arthurian legends" (121). Yet this "battle" is quite differently understood than it is cast in the *Slate* article. For one, the ticks themselves are granted their own "quest," and for another, the struggle is put in evolutionary terms, with the buildup of innumerable "lifetimes"—and therefore none of the reductive, singular "authoring" that Alaimo calls attention to. In Haskell's rendering, humans jostle with ticks, and might be more mindful of the overlaps and folds that exist between species.

I'm not writing about this from an abstract intellectual vantage point, or at some academic remove. As I write this I'm sitting on the hilltop in northern Michigan, within a pine grove where many ticks pass through on a daily basis. I've plucked over a dozen ticks off my clothes this year, and have removed three from Julien's skin, two from Camille's, and four from my own. Last week I found a tick crawling across one of our pillows. Each evening Lara and I try to do a thorough tick check on our children's bodies, as well as on each other. On nights that we're too busy and forget to check, I'll wake up in a sweat, worried that I most certainly have a tick lodged in me somewhere. So far, I've been lucky—but my luck could run out at any time. This is all to say that I live with a grounded knowledge and even a genuine fear of ticks; I'm not diminishing their reality or threats.

But when I read things like the *Slate* article, or hear people denigrate ticks wholesale as an evil species that should be eliminated, I can't help but detect disturbing if scaled-down echoes of racist, xenophobic, nationalist, or otherwise hateful tirades—the sort of language and sentiments that fuel reprehensible acts of violence and political impasses. These things are not helping our species sustain life on the planet, for humans or anyone (or anything) else. While I'm not at all sure that humans have final agency on this question of biospheric balance, it does seem clear that people have the ability to inflect more or less violence, at multiple scales.

I'm not proposing that there are straightforward ways to deal with ticks, once and for all. It's work, constant and constantly unsettling. Ticks don't recognize property lines or the human distinction between inside and outside. Lyme disease can be crippling, even fatal. However, ticks might draw us into more long-term, thought-provoking negotiations with and among other species and our surroundings. They are, for better and worse, one part of our intricate, continually unfolding planetary ecosystem— and, like any species, ticks cannot be excised in one fell swoop without vast (if perhaps subtle, at first) ripple effects. To borrow the words of Donna Haraway from her latest book *Staying with the Trouble*, "Neither the critters nor the people could have existed or could endure without each other in ongoing, curious practices" (133). I'm interested in our ongoing practices with ticks—again, acknowledging that these practices are complex, and vexed by interactive violence on both sides.

I like Haraway's emphasis of "staying," because really we're talking about temporality, about how people are so often in too much of a rush to be attentive to the world they are passing through—and living in—all the time. Staying with the trouble of ticks means living with them, dealing with them, being *attentive* to them. This is neither easy to grasp in theory, nor easy to put into practice. It means flicking them off, sometimes, or other times simply watching them pass by. Sometimes it might mean removing a tick from your skin and crushing it between two rocks, or pinching it dead in the teeth of pliers. It means paying attention to ticks, to recognizing them as a part of this world—an awkward part, no doubt, but still no less a part than, well, than anything else.

As I finish this essay Julien is pulling on my arm, asking me to go for a walk in the woods to hunt for chanterelle mushrooms. With all the rain we've had in June we're experiencing a bumper crop of the delicious, apricot-smelling fungus. These golden mushrooms like to grow around oak trees, and this year they are popping up among the countless decomposing acorns beneath the northern red oaks in our woods. Two years ago was a "mast year" for the oaks, which means that they dropped all their acorns early. The mass of acorns becomes a boon for the mice the following winter, who survive, thrive, and propagate thanks to the bounty of abundant acorn meat. With more mice scurrying through the woods this year, ticks have more warm-blooded bodies to latch onto. We live in these woods, with the oaks, chanterelles, mice, and ticks—among innumerable other species and things. This is tick thinking, and it doesn't stop here. It's ongoing.

Dark river balloon

End of summer, back in New Orleans. One morning soon after we return, I'm not really sure why, I head for the river at the perfectly unreasonable hour of 4:30 a.m. As I walk through the silent neighborhoods cast in eerie streetlight glow, I catch glimpses of countless cats slinking and darting under cars, and I witness the death of Santa Claus: an uncannily life-size plastic St. Nicholas figurine in a trash can, head poking out. It occurs to me that I have set out far too early. It won't be light for an hour and a half. What the hell am I doing here?

My path to the river skirts the edge of the zoo, and a pungent waft of giraffe dung envelops me. An eerie wail issues repeatedly from somewhere deep in the zoo as I stroll along the outer fence. The walk has been bizarre enough up to this point, and the zoo sounds tip things farther in that direction—it's depressing, and I am tempted to turn around and walk straight home. Even as I head toward the wild fish of the murky Mississippi, the zoo reminds me of the words of Randy Malamud, concerning how "little space remains in our minds to consider any animals besides these weird ones foregrounded in our cultural frames" ("Vengeful Tiger, Glowing Rabbit").

I am conflicted about my fishing excursions, and I go through periods where I feel uncertain about whether to continue fishing or not. I try to practice ethical catch-and-release protocols and careful handling of the fish; still, it's hard to get around the baseline violence of forcibly embedding a hook in another creature's mouth. But I'm too close to the river now, and anyway I have a new eight-weight fly rod that I am excited to try. My old five-weight, which I bought in Driggs, Idaho, seventeen years ago, is really better suited to trout streams and small ponds.

When I get to the river it is ridiculously dark. I can't even see well enough to tie a fly to my line. It's nearly pitch black, but I can tell that the river has dropped a couple feet; I don't recognize the same place where I fished a week ago. I'm tentative about wading into unfamiliar water while it's still so dark. It's not even five o'clock yet. There is a lot of boat activity, though: tankers and tugboats chug by, and distant *boings* and *clangs* echo from the docks across the river. I sit down on the riprap and assemble my rod slowly in the dark. I look across the dark river, and I think back on the zoo.

One of the books that my children love to read before bedtime is a zoo story called "Goodnight Gorilla." The basic story is that a zookeeper puts all the animals to bed one by one, and a gorilla (the first to be put to bed) gets hold of the keys and lets all the animals back out of their cages as the sleepy and unknowing zookeeper goes about his business. The animals orchestrate a surprise toward the end.

There's also an embedded subplot located in a seemingly innocuous object, a red balloon that, if you look closely, a mouse is untying from the cage bars on the first page. Over the course of the book the balloon drifts away, yet it appears on every page hovering on the horizon in some part of each scene. This is not the red balloon of the eponymous film from 1956. In that story, the red balloon *is* the story, and it guides the action and drama. That French red balloon becomes a friend, an accomplice, and a sustained flight of fancy.

The red balloon in *Goodnight Gorilla*, on the other hand, is just *there*. It's just hanging in every page, getting smaller but always existing—if sometimes only apparent by its black dangling string. It occurred to me, sitting there in the dark, that the river is more like *this* balloon than the balloon in *The Red Balloon*. The Mississippi is just *there*, and always going away. It slips by seemingly endlessly, whether you focus on it or not. It winds around the city, *above* the city even—this realization hits you sometimes when you're walking down the street in New Orleans and you have a view down toward the river, and you see the bulkhead of a tanker cruising by weirdly overhead. I'm scheduled to teach children's literature next semester, and so these things are on my mind: how to show the work of literature as it spans across ages, spaces, and times.

It's finally almost light out, so I scramble down to the river.

This morning becomes more of a scavenging project than anything else. The fish aren't as active as the last time I was here, and with the river level down a lot of mucky bank is exposed. I discover all sorts of things, from a beached blue crab to a machined-looking thing, some part of some apparatus long since rendered inoperable.

I fish for a while, but I don't catch anything. I get the hang of my new outfit, though: enjoying the hiss of fresh fly line shooting through the rod's eyelets. Before my buddy Brian shows up, it's just me and two bitterns stealthily stalking fish in the shallows. Mostly I find myself feeling overwhelmed by the mass of moving water, aware of its magnitude, muddiness, and beauty—but also wary of the limits of my own awareness of the river. Heraclitus said you can't step in the same river twice; I'm not sure if you can even step into a river *once* as a discrete, knowable thing.

The work of literature in an age of post-truth involves this clumsy, awkward getting to know places—the places from which narratives emerge, and where they swerve and become unfamiliar.

Landscape ecology

I want to return to that November evening in 2013, when I went canoeing with the Environment Program at Loyola. I need to say more about this experience, as in so many ways it epitomized the liberal arts at its peak, both in terms of practical lessons and as indescribable *jouissance*. I try to teach my students that so much of effective reading involves *re*reading, and writing can involve rewriting, too. The work of literature involves reworking literature—not letting things be easily settled.

And so I recall that afternoon when we drove in vans west out of New Orleans, to where I-55 heads north toward Memphis. On a narrow stretch of marshy ground between Maurepas Swamp and Lake Pontchartrain, we pulled off the frontage road and loaded into twelve canoes. As we set out, we had to paddle under the elevated highway. This was a strange, fantastical experience: to be slipping through the shimmering calm water, past enormous concrete pilings as cars and trucks went hurtling by twenty or so feet above.

Making our way into Shell Bank Bayou, we paused to discuss the invasive Chinese tallow trees that grow along the boggy edges of the water. David White (now retired from Loyola; I miss him) explained how they were imported as ornamental plants (they are in the same family as the seasonally available, flashy red poinsettia), and how their waxy seed casings serve as food for various bird species. The birds, having eaten the outer husks, let the seeds themselves drop all over—and over time, spreading these trees everywhere. Their seeds can lay dormant in the ground for up to seven years, waiting until a storm knocks down grown trees, allowing direct sunlight to hit the ground, whereupon the seeds finally germinate.

The water moved around us gently but steadily—it's still water, yet there are subtle currents: you'd notice it when clumps of spinning water hyacinths would come barreling by, drawn somewhere into the bayou faster than the canoe. Deeper into the bayou, we came across the rusted metal structure of an old fishing camp—another reminder of the human presence that helped shape this landscape.

As night fell, we all formed a loose flotilla in a dense marshy area surrounded by cattails and cypress stands. David gave his brief talk on "landscape ecology," touching on the "idea of wilderness," crepuscular species, noise pollution, sensory overload, and how our bodies become more relaxed out here. It was really great: everyone quietly slapping and shooing away the mosquitoes that were suddenly swarming us, but still listening—relaxing. We could hear the shush of the highway in the distance, and the eerie hoot-hoots of owls as they swooped through the cypress trees.

What really stuck with me was David's mention of *scale* as a key landscape-ecological term, and it made me think about what we had been doing in my literature and environment courses that semester.

For instance, that same week when we discussed Brenda Hillman's poem "Symmetry Breaking," we looked at how the lines shift scale radically as the air traveler speaker reflects on various parts of the cosmos that assert themselves as her plane cruises above the north American continent. The focus moves from the airplane meal in front of the speaker, the "chicken with/the flap of itself on top" and the "triangle of Cool Whip," to the vast landscape of Utah unfurling out the window, and even to the universe in some distant moment when it "said goodbye to evenness" (54). The poem ponders the bizarrely workaday airline food and dull airport rituals while also assessing vast reaches of time and space—we are presented with overlapping and interpenetrating "landscapes" that foreground different forms of life and nonlife. We can't be too quick to deem which came "first" or determine what is the more "natural" here; instead, we are called on to consider closely the patterns of movement and behavior at different levels, from "cell division" to the "dinner roll."

During his talk about landscape ecology, David referred to certain places like the Grand Canyon, where the idea of wilderness is more palpable; but he said even when camping there, he recalled seeing the flashing lights of jets 30,000 feet above. I remembered that experience too: being at the bottom of the canyon, lying next to the rumble of Hermit Rapids at night, and seeing the tiny blink blink blink blink way above me. This was like an inverted version of Brenda Hillman's poem, with the riparian ecosystem in the foreground and the little interior world of the airliner far removed, but nevertheless weirdly present and evident. These are some of the things that landscape ecology considers: the distances and gaps between things, and yet the connections and overlaps, where they exist—and how these can change over time. It's a way of thinking about processes on multiple scales, at once.

Heading home after dusk, we passed again beneath the towering strip of highway, and it was even more surreal in the pitch black of night—the aerial headlights and warped whooshes like some ongoing alien enterprise bisecting the bayou. Or maybe *we* were the aliens: David had told us that as we paddled back to the launch site we would be overwhelmed by the sounds of the highway, and he was right. It was hard to imagine that we'd soon be on a similar corridor, rushing back to New Orleans through the night.

Back in the classroom

After my long year away, after reflecting on teaching literature and my place in this disorienting era of post-truth, I find myself back in the classroom. My first semester back at Loyola I'm teaching two first-year seminars and an upper level class on the environmental humanities. Course caps were raised over the summer with barely any acknowledgment of the effect on actual classes, and this means my "seminars" have crept up over the years from fifteen to twenty then twenty-five students—which is hardly a *seminar* at all. But still, I try to make it work.

These first-year seminars are meant to help freshmen students adjust to college, while also giving them some disciplinary skills as well as a glimpse into a certain field or topic. Offered by faculty across the university, they are on topics from digital media to incarceration, from the US constitution to the history of New Orleans, and from diversity in society to the philosophy of sports. My seminar is called "Interpreting Airports." Starting with Richard Scarry's *A Day at the Airport*, we discuss how airports work and what feelings, assumptions, and associations they rely on. We read short stories and poems that involve airports, and we consider a variety of essays and news articles and look at visual culture, too.

Very early in the semester, I begin one class by telling my freshmen about this book that I'm trying to finish, *The Work of Literature in an Age of Post-Truth*. I ask them if they've heard the phrase "post-truth"—and not a single student has. More students have heard the expression "alternative facts," and even more pipe up when I ask about "fake news." We talk about how this phrase in particular is strange, for how it can be wielded deceptively just as it can be used to accurately describe something. I tell them how these concepts are related to the idea of "post-truth," and I mention that it was *Oxford*

Dictionary's "word of the year" last year. A student scoffs, "Wait, there's a *word of the year?!*"

I bring the discussion back around to literature. So what does literature have to do with this? What even *is* literature? Students offer up some answers: literature is *stories*; literature is *writing*; literature is *texts*. OK, but so what is the *work* of literature, especially in a time when we as a culture can seem uncertain if not outright dubious about the truth-function of language, in all these things we've mentioned (stories, writing, texts)?

We shift gears—slow down—and look at a poem together. First thing's first: I ask a student to read the poem aloud. Then, I ask another student to read it aloud, a second time. The poem is Elly Bookman's "Privilege," and it reverberates intensely with its planes flying "low and heavy, back and / forth from the base, / practicing war." This poem is set around an ambiguous air force base, but commercial airliners also frame the poem, as "small whitenesses passing/like tired stars/through the blue." My students are aware that even as we read this poem, US bombers are flying in threatening formation around North Korea, and that a new travel ban is being rolled out at airports around the country. Also at this same moment, Puerto Rico's San Juan airport is jammed with people trying to get home, get out, get anywhere beyond the hurricane devastated island. A few days prior a popular image had circulated around the Internet, which tracked private flights headed toward the Caribbean as the commercial airliners were all flying away: these private jets were flying *into* the storm to bring the wealthy out. What *is* privilege in this strange time? At the end of class, a student comes up to me and suggests that I read the poem again with an alternative point of view in mind: maybe the *airport* is the speaker. It's a stretch but a good impulse, to imagine the perceptive capacities of things beyond the human. It's environmental studies with no limits, again.

A week later we are discussing Sherman Alexie's short story "Flight Patterns." While written as a distinctly post-9/11 story, it seems more poignant than ever with its send-up of racial prejudices and crisscrossed lines of commercial travel and military power, and their corollary diasporas. Our in-class discussions brim with the charged feelings of the moment, which is at once thrilling and jolting—sending us out of airports and into politics, history, and questions of social justice.

In my other class I am teaching Octavia Butler's *Dawn* again, but in a different context—thinking with my students about how the novel puts pressure on our notions of environment, ecology, and evolution. With the threat of nuclear catastrophe "back on the table," as it were, my students are riveted by Octavia Butler's post-human scenarios not just as fantasy but also as an almost wistful alternative to final planetary annihilation. A couple days later, Margret Grebowicz's book *The National Park to Come* poses new questions for us as Trump's administration considers shrinking national monuments and rolling back environmental regulations.

It's a new and strange time to be doing the work of literature, by turns anxious making and urgent feeling—more detached than ever, and yet exactly what we (me, my students) need. To linger over things, dwell together, to *not* jump to conclusions or merely seethe internally (or externally). At the same time, number crunching committees on my campus are demanding clearer and concrete learning outcomes, assessment rubrics, and data sets. It's a paradoxical position: I want to preserve the *freeplay* of the humanities classrooms and I think this is more important than ever, but the ineffable and incalculable qualities of such an education make it a target for revamping, if not outright elimination.

I can't help but think of another text that I frequently teach in my Twentieth-Century American Fiction course, Donald Barthelme's short story "The Balloon." As the narrator of this odd tale explains the makeup and function of the eponymous gargantuan object, it brushes against these unfortunately still very modern demands:

> The amount of specialized training currently needed, and the consequent desirability of long-term commitments, has been occasioned by the steadily growing importance of complex machinery, in virtually all kinds of operations; as this tendency increases, more and more people will turn, in bewildered inadequacy, to solutions for which the balloon may stand as a prototype, or "rough draft." (51)

This passage reminds me of how people look to college right now as something that should abet and explain contemporary culture, and result in a finite value—rather than appreciate it as an utterly different sort of exception to these as-if rules. Drawing students into the slow, uncertain experience of literary reading—this is *not* a definitive job skill, even if it teaches patience, flexibility, and creative thinking. It's something I want to keep doing alongside of and against the viral nature of fake news and alternative facts, precisely because it is critically grounding—even as it ungrounds long held assumptions and common sense. If college cannot be justified perfectly economically or in terms of Achieved Progress, then all the better. It is not a "rough draft" for modern adult life, but a place where we might fully be, and fully re-imagine things altogether—and for the better.

I think about these things as I walk home from campus, seeing people text madly on their phones in their cars as they race down St. Charles Avenue, and as aircraft on final approach into Louis Armstrong International Airport adjust their flaps overhead.

Back home I notice that a storm has ripped the main electrical line bracket off the decayed siding on a corner of my house, just beneath the roof. There have been heavy rains this fall as record temperatures have heated up the ocean and gulf and produced big blooming cumulous clouds heavy with precipitation, as well as multiple hurricanes. I put in a call to the power company to get their help, since it involves the electrical grid and is beyond my expertise. In the back room of my house I spot another problem: the rain is soaking through a rotted piece of wood in the window frame. This fix I can do, at least temporarily. I scrape and patch the rotted section of wood, then attach some steel flashing to hang over the sill so as to redirect the rainwater away, using my pliers to bend down the sharp corners of the flashing so Julien and Camille won't gouge themselves as they pass by. This is a short-term repair but hopefully enough to get us through the winter. Anyway, I have my classes to think about, and rereading to do.

EPILOGUE

This book has meandered over a wide range of subjects—moving from literary passages to daily walks, from wilderness adventures to academic musings, and from questions of ecology to the in-between realms of air travel.

How is this all captured under the gauze of *the work of literature*? It is something of a network. For me this book has been a way to account for the recurrent things that I think about and work on in proximity to literature. I teach college courses on literary texts and writing, and my interests beyond the classroom filter back into this space and shape what I teach and write about. So my classes—within my thankfully fuzzy home discipline of English—have come to include airports, contemporary culture, and environmental thought. And, in turn, my students push me to reconsider my own attachments to these extraliterary things and activities—and so I approach them afresh.

In this age of post-truth, when narratives move disturbingly fast and can be warped to disgusting political ends with grave implications on the ground, traditional literature and the skills that come with it might seem aloof, quaint, even obsolete. But these things are more important than ever: being able to read slowly, to carefully consider how narratives are fabricated, produced, disseminated, and consumed—and the weight (if not exactly *truth*) that people give these narratives, for however long or quickly. These considerations have to be informed by broader interests, by a wider world of things. If there is an upshot to dwelling in an age of post-truth, it might mean that we can traverse hard distinctions, undo borders, and, to put it simply, be more *creative*.

The work of literature right now is about including more material in our canons and discussions, about fanning out into the world. I try to do this in my teaching, and I've attempted something like this here in these pages. This book is about how my interests have incubated, developed, intersected, dispersed, and lingered over many years—all the while intermingled with the teaching of literature.

Oftentimes one's scholarly expertise can be understood as strictly academic—that is, not translating to daily life. This book has been my endeavor to push against this, to show how myriad objects of curiosity comingle, on campus as well as in terminals and along riverbanks. This book is hardly a neat and tidy model, and it doesn't exactly have a heuristic function. Nevertheless, I hope it inspires others to weave together their interests in and out of the classroom, and to follow them over many years. The work of literature is a long game (even allowing that "game" is not a great metaphor). The contents of this book have been drawn from eight years of teaching at Loyola, living in New Orleans, traveling, parenting, writing, reflecting on higher education, spending time in the north woods of my childhood home, and getting back into the classroom.

Our age of post-truth is also an age of rabid compartmentalization, where people's beliefs, aesthetics, consumer habits, transportation modes, and politics are all too frequently cordoned off from one another. We need to push against this, to make connections: which is *not* the same as saying simply and with a shrug that "everything is connected." The work of literature can risk totalizing: think of how a novel can conjure a whole world, and how literary lessons can be recklessly interpreted to be universal. But the work of literature might also present ways to think across *different* things—if not to totalize, then to see amalgams, disjunctions, and murky areas of overlap and co-shaping. And to see these things as at once personal and collective, both sweeping across the planet and taking shape in local sites at each instant.

I felt the need to write a few words by way of conclusion, about how this book's heterogeneous contents interact—or at least, how I see them interacting in my mind, especially as I find myself back in the classroom in this perplexing time. The work of literature in an age of post-truth goes way beyond the book, past readers and writers and into and through the world all around. And I don't mean this to sound like an impossibly capacious definition. Rather, it means that nothing is off limits. It's a place to start from again and again, without a foreseeable end.

ACKNOWLEDGMENTS

Thanks to my editor Haaris Naqvi at Bloomsbury for ongoing support and friendship. Thank you to Emily Jane Cohen for incisive feedback on an early draft of this book. I'm grateful to have had a wonderful student assistant, Leah Shain, who helped me hone the book and rearrange chapters. My colleagues at Loyola University New Orleans keep me upbeat and appreciating the work of literature each day on our campus, even when things look bleak. Thanks especially to Hillary Eklund and Mark Yakich for inspiring significant parts of this book. Ed Winstead, Sarah Bray, David Winters, Eileen Joy, Michael Marder, Linda Levitt, Rob Horning, and Jonathan Hahn gave superb editorial advice and suggestions on pieces from the book that were published in earlier forms in *Guernica*, *Public Books*, *Inside Higher Ed*, *3:AM Magazine*, *O-Zone*, *The Philosophical Salon*, *The New Everyday*, *Real Life*, and *Sierra*. Thank you Susan Clements for indexing. Thanks, finally, to my family, Lara, Julien, and Camille for boundless love and generosity as we've attempted to make a life around the strange work of literature—at times amorphous and consuming, but I hope enriching and stimulating, too.

BIBLIOGRAPHY

Agamben, Giorgio. *The Open: Man and Animal*. Edited by Kevin Attell. Stanford: Stanford University Press, 2004.

Alaimo, Stacy. *Exposed: Environmental Politics and Pleasures in Posthuman Times*. Minneapolis: University of Minnesota Press, 2016.

Alexie, Sherman. "Flight Patterns." In *Ten Little Indians*. New York: Grove Press, 2004.

Baldwin, James. *Giovanni's Room*. New York: Vintage International, 2013.

Barthelme, Donald. "The Balloon." In *Sixty Stories*. Edited by David Gates. London: Penguin Classics, 2003.

Barthes, Roland. *Mythologies*. New York: Hill and Wang, 1972.

Barthes, Roland. "The Death of the Author." In *Image, Music, Text*. Edited by Stephen Heath. New York: Hill and Wang, 2009.

Bean, John C. *Engaging Ideas: The Professor's Guide to Integrating Writing, Critical Thinking, and Active Learning in the Classroom*. Hoboken: Wiley, 2011.

Benjamin, Walter. "The Work of Art in the Age of Mechanical Reproduction." In *Illuminations*. Harcourt Brace Jovanovich, Inc., 1968.

Bogost, Ian. *Alien Phenomenology, Or, What It's Like to Be a Thing*. Minneapolis: University of Minnesota Press, 2012.

Bonkoski, Jon. "Mapping Wetlands." Personal email received by Christopher Schaberg, *Mapping Wetlands*, February 16, 2017.

Butler, Octavia E. *Dawn*. New York: Warner Books, 1997.

Chopin, Kate. "The Story of an Hour." In *The Complete Works of Kate Chopin*. Baton Rouge: Louisiana State University Press, 2006.

Davis, Lydia. "Strange Impulse." In *Varieties of Disturbance: Stories*. New York: Farrar, Straus & Giroux, 2007.

DeLillo, Don. *White Noise*. New York: Penguin, 1986.

DeLillo, Don. "Midnight in Dostoevsky." In *The Angel Esmeralda: Nine Stories*. New York: Scribner, 2012.

Eklund, Hilary. "Swamp Things." Personal email received by Christopher Schaberg, *Swamp Things*, February 16, 2017.

Emerson, Ralph Waldo. *Nature and Selected Essays*. Edited by Larzer Ziff. New York: Penguin, 2003.

Fanon, Frantz. "The Lived Experience of a Black Man." In *The Routledge Critical and Cultural Theory Reader*. Edited by Neil Badmington and Julia Thomas. New York: Routledge, 2008.

Fitzgerald, F. Scott. *The Last Tycoon*. New York: Charles Scribner's Sons, 1980.

Foucault, Michel. "What Is an Author?" In *Aesthetics, Method, and Epistemology*. New York: The New Press, 2006.

Grebowicz, Margret. *The National Park to Come*. Stanford: Stanford University Press, 2015.

Haraway, Donna. *Staying with the Trouble*. Durham: Duke University Press, 2016.

Haskell, David George. *The Forest Unseen*. New York: Penguin, 2013.

Heidegger, Martin. *Being and Time*. Oxford, UK: Blackwell, 2013.

Hemingway, Ernest. "Big Two Hearted River." In *The Complete Short Stories of Ernest Hemingway*. New York: Scribner, 2007.

Hemingway, Ernest. *A Moveable Feast*. New York: Scribner, 2010.

Hemingway, Ernest. *The Old Man and the Sea*. Oxford: Benedict Classics, 2016.

Hillman, Brenda. "Breaking Symmetry." In *Loose Sugar*. Hanover, NH: University of New England Press, 1997.

Jameson, Fredric. *The Political Unconscious: Narrative as a Socially Symbolic Act*. Ithaca: Cornell University Press, 1994.

Jewett, Sarah Orne. "Bold Words at the Bridge." In *The Irish Stories of Sarah Orne Jewett*. Edited by Jack Morgan. Carbondale, IL: Southern Illinois University Press, 2002.

Kasarda, John D., and Greg Lindsay. *Aerotropolis*. New York: Farrar, Straus & Giroux, 2011.

Li, Yiyun. *The Vagrants*. New York: Random House, 2009.

Mandel, Emily St. John. *Station Eleven: A Novel*. New York: Knopf Doubleday Group, 2014.

Manguso, Sarah. *300 Arguments*. Minneapolis: Graywolf, 2017.

Marx, Karl. "A Contribution to the Critique of Political Economy." In *The Routledge Critical and Cultural Theory Reader*. Edited by Neil Badmington and Julia Thomas. New York: Routledge, 2008.

McCarthy, Cormac. *The Road*. New York: Random House, 2006.

McLuhan, Marshall. *Understanding Media: The Extensions of Man*. Corte Madera, CA: Gingko Press, 2011.

Morton, Timothy. *The Ecological Thought*. Cambridge, MA; London: Harvard University Press, 2012.

Morton, Timothy. *Hyperobjects: Philosophy and Ecology After the End of the World*. Minneapolis: University of Minnesota Press, 2014.

Nabokov, Vladimir. *Lolita*. New York: Random House, 1998.

Nelson, Maggie. *The Argonauts*. Minneapolis: Graywolf, 2016.

Nietzsche, Friedrich Wilhelm. *The Birth of Tragedy and the Genealogy of Morals*. Translated by Francs Golffing. New York: Doubleday & Co., 1956.

Nietzsche, Friedrich Wilhelm. "94." In *Beyond Good and Evil: Prelude to a Philosophy of the Future*. Edited by Walter Arnold Kaufmann. New York: Vintage Books, 2011.

O'Connor, Flannery. "A Good Man is Hard to Find." In *A Good Man Is Hard to Find and Other Stories*. Boston, MA: Houghton Mifflin Harcourt, 1976.

Pynchon, Thomas. *The Crying of Lot 49*. New York: Harper Perennial, 2009.

Riott, Kristin. "Re: New Airport; Environmental Impact." Personal email received by Christopher Schaberg, *Re: New Airport; Environmental Impact*. July 11, 2017.

Scott, A. O. "'The End of the Tour' Offers a Tale of Two Davids." Rev. of The End of The Tour. *The New York Times*, July 30, 2015.

Sommer, Robert. *Tight Spaces: Hard Architecture and How to Humanize It*. Englewood Cliffs, NJ: Spectrum, 1974.

Stein, Gertrude. *Tender Buttons and Three Lives*. New York: Signet, 2003.

Thoreau, Henry David. *The Maine Woods*. New York: Penguin, 1988.

Toomer, Jean. *Cane*. New York: Liveright, 2011.

Tsing, Anna Lowenhaupt. *The Mushroom at the End of the World: On the Possibility of Life in Capitalist Ruins*. Princeton, NJ: Princeton University Press, 2015.

Twain, Mark. *Life On the Mississippi*. New York: Penguin Books, 1984.

Wallace, David Foster. *This Is Water: Some Thoughts, Delivered on a Significant Occasion, about Living a Compassionate Life*. New York: Little Brown and Company, 2009.

Wallace, David Foster. *The Pale King: An Unfinished Novel*. New York: Back Bay, 2012.

Williams, Raymond. "Culture is Ordinary." In *The Routledge Critical and Cultural Theory Reader*. Edited by Neil Badmington and Julia Thomas. New York: Routledge, 2008.

Web Resources

Ahmed, Sara. "Against Students." *The New Inquiry*. June 2015. https://thenewinquiry.com/against-students/ (Accessed October 25, 2017.)

"Airports and KCI." Interview by Gina Kaufmann, Mathew Long-Middleton, Christopher Schaberg, Daniel Serda, Michael Mackie, and Cat Mahari. *KCUR 89.3*. 15 June 2017. Web. October 18, 2017. http://kcur.org/post/airports-and-kci#stream/0 (Accessed October 25, 2017.)

Alloa, Emmanuel. "Post-Truth Or: Why Nietzsche Is Not Responsible
for Donald Trump." *The Philosophical Salon* (a *Los Angeles Review
of Books* channel), September 09, 2017. http://thephilosophicalsalon.
com/post-truth-or-why-nietzsche-is-not-responsible-for-donald-trump/
(Accessed October 25, 2017.)

Bogost, Ian. "Hyperemployment, or the Exhausting Work of the
Technology User." *The Atlantic*, November 08, 2013. www.theatlantic.
com/technology/archive/2013/11/hyperemployment-or-the-exhausting-
work-of-the-technology-user/281149/ (Accessed October 25, 2017).

Bookman, Elly. "Privilege." *The New Yorker*. August 21, 2017. www.
newyorker.com/magazine/2017/08/21/privilege-elly-bookman
(Accessed October 25, 2017).

Greer, Andrew Sean. "It's A Summer Day." *The New Yorker*. June 19,
2017. www.newyorker.com/magazine/2017/06/19/its-a-summer-day
(Accessed October 25, 2017.)

Hawthorne, Christopher. "Building Type: The Airport as Public Square
and Protest Central." *Los Angeles Times*. February 2, 2017. http://
www.latimes.com/entertainment/arts/la-ca-cm-building-type-4-2017-
02-05-story.html (Accessed October 25, 2017.)

"*How The World Is Responding to Trump's Travel Ban.*"
Digital image. *The Washington Post*. https://2.bp.blogspot.
com/-TftQfBTdS6s/WJHkhrp6-GI/AAAAAAAADS8/
zac8sqqD3TwT8TMr2wRmeChtG9BqdUEZgCLcB/s1600/
points%2Bof%2Bdetention.PNG (Accessed October 25, 2017.)

@KatieKMCO. https://twitter.com/KatieKCMO/
status/875387371881189377 (Accessed July 25, 2017.)

Kenny, Glenn. "Why The End of the Tour Isn't Really about My Friend
David Foster Wallace." Rev. of The End of the Tour. *The Guardian*.
July 29, 2015. https://www.theguardian.com/books/2015/jul/29/why-
the-end-of-the-tour-isnt-really-about-my-friend-david-foster-wallace
(Accessed October 25, 2017.)

"Lilette." *Travel + Leisure*. http://www.travelandleisure.com/travel-guide/
new-orleans/restaurants/lilette (Accessed October 25, 2017.)

Malady, Matthew J.X. "The Useless Agony of Going Offline." *The New
Yorker*. January 27, 2016. https://www.newyorker.com/books/page-
turner/the-useless-agony-of-going-offline (Accessed October 25, 2017.)

Malamud, Randy. "Vengeful Tiger, Glowing Rabbit." *The Chronicle of
Higher Education*. http://www.chronicle.com/article/Vengeful-Tiger-
Glowing-Rabbit/132951 (Accessed October 25, 2017.)

Mele, Christopher. "Man Kicked J.F.K. Airport Worker Wearing Hijab,
Prosecutor Says." *The New York Times*. January 26, 2017. www.
nytimes.com/2017/01/26/nyregion/queens-ny-jfk-attack.html (Accessed
October 25, 2017.)

Miley, Mike. "The Eye of Sauron David Foster Wallace and the Interview."
    Just Words. July 18, 2015. https://medium.com/just-words/the-eye-of-
    sauron-d454ed83377a (Accessed October 25, 2017.)
"Mission Statement." *Hillsdale College*. https://www.hillsdale.edu/about/
    mission/ (Accessed October 25, 2017.
Moore, Lorrie. "Childcare." *The New Yorker*. July 13, 2009. www.
    newyorker.com/magazine/2009/07/06/childcare (Accessed October 25,
    2017.)
Moyer, Melinda Wenner. "The Year of the Tick." *Slate Magazine*. June 26,
    2017. www.slate.com/articles/life/the_kids/2017/06/how_to_prevent_
    tick_bites_and_lyme_disease_during_the_tick_threat_of_2017.html.
    (Accessed October 25, 2017.)
"#OccupyAirports on Twitter." *Twitter*, April 29, 2017, https://twitter.
    com/hashtag/OccupyAirports?src=hash (Accessed October 25, 2017.)
O'Connor, Stephen. "Ziggurat." *The New Yorker*. June 19, 2017. https://
    www.newyorker.com/magazine/2009/06/29/ziggurat (Accessed
    October 25, 2017.)
Remes, Jacob. "Key Sites of Employment (often the Biggest Worksite
    in a City), Surveillance, Migration, and Movement of Goods
    and People." *Twitter*. January 29, 2017, twitter.com/jacremes/
    status/825543514494742529. (Accessed October 25, 2017.)
Remnick, David. "Obama Reckons with a Trump Presidency."
    The New Yorker. November 28, 2016, www.newyorker.com/
    magazine/2016/11/28/obama-reckons-with-a-trump-presidency
    (Accessed October 25, 2017.)
Selingo, Jeffrey, Richard Ekman, Victor Ferrall, and Catharine Bond Hill.
    "Worries About the Future of Liberal Arts Colleges." Interview by
    Diane Rehm. Audio blog post. The Diane Rehm Show. National Public
    Radio. March 19, 2015. https://dianerehm.org/shows/2015-03-19/
    worries-about-the-future-of-liberal-arts-colleges (Accessed October 25,
    2017.)
Shechtman, Anna. "David Foster Wallace's Closed Circuit." Rev. of The
    End of the Tour. 25 July 2015. *Los Angeles Review of Books*. https://
    lareviewofbooks.org/article/david-foster-wallaces-closed-circuit-the-
    end-of-the-tour/ (Accessed October 25, 2017.)
Shephard, Alex. "Donald Trump Doesn't Read Books." *New Republic*.
    2016. https://newrepublic.com/minutes/133566/donald-trump-doesnt-
    read-books (Accessed October 25, 2017.)
Tanz, Jason. "Consider the Movie About the Book About David Foster
    Wallace." Rev. of The End of the Tour. *Wired* July 29, 2015. Wired.
    https://www.wired.com/2015/07/david-foster-wallace-end-of-the-tour/
    (Accessed October 25, 2017.)

Travel Ban Protest Image. Digital image. *Business Insider*. https://static5.
businessinsider.com/image/588e1676713ba1e81c8b5142-2400/
undefined (Accessed October 25, 2017.)
"What is Critical Thinking?" University of Louisville, Ideas to Action
(i2a). http://louisville.edu/ideastoaction/about/criticalthinking/what
(Accessed October 25, 2017.)
"Wilderness." *The Oxford English Dictionary*. http://www.oed.com/view/
Entry/229003?redirectedFrom=wilderness#eid (Accessed October 25,
2017.)

Films

22 Jump Street. Directed by Phil Lord and Chris Miller. New Orleans,
LA: Columbia Pictures, 2014.
Birdman. Directed by Alejandro Gonzalez Iñárritu. New York City, NY:
Fox Searchlight, 2014.
Kung Fu Panda. Directed by Mark Osborne and John Stevenson.
Glendale, CA: DreamWorks Animation SKG, 2008.
Labyrinth. Directed by Jim Henson. Haverstraw, NY: Lucasfilm, 1986.
Liberal Arts. Directed by Josh Radnor. Gambier, OH: BCDF Pictures and
Strategic Motion Ventures, 2012.
Miami Vice. Directed by Michael Mann. Miami, FL: Universal Pictures,
2006.
Stranger Things. Matt Duffer and Ross Duffer, creators. 21 Laps
Entertainment and Monkey Massacre, 2016.
The Big Lebowski. Directed by Joel Coen and Ethan Coen. Beverly Hills,
CA: Polygram Filmed Entertainment, 1998.
The End of the Tour. Directed by James Ponsolt. Boston, MA: Modern
Man Films, 2015.
The Matrix. Directed by Lana Wachowski and Lilly Wachowski. Sydney,
New South Wales: Warner Bros., 1999.
Willy Wonka & the Chocolate Factory. Directed by Mel Stuart. Munich,
West Germany: Paramount Pictures, 1971.

INDEX

liberal arts. *See* literature and literary studies
Life on the Mississippi (Twain) 8, 10–11
Lipsky, David 79, 80, 82
literature and literary studies
  airports 42–5, 77, 85, 91, 114, 115, 117, 122, 124–5, 138–9, 143
  aphorisms 92–4
  careerism 48–52
  civility 42–5
  consumerism 31–4, 52–3, 59, 64, 80
  contemporary culture 1, 3, 5, 23–34, 79, 80, 143–4
  ecology and environment 8, 10–11, 12, 20–1, 29, 46, 65, 107, 108, 120–1, 130–3, 134–5, 137, 138, 140, 143
  film 34–6, 60, 79–81, 83–4
  liberal arts 2, 4, 16–17, 50, 58, 59–62, 71, 72, 75–6, 79, 95–100
  and life 5, 7, 14–20, 21, 31–4, 48–52, 58, 71, 80, 143–4
  perspectivism 11–13
  place and space 2, 22, 25, 27, 30, 45–7, 76–8, 117
  politics 11, 23–4, 27–8, 36
  slowness 21, 23, 27, 28, 36, 70
  storytelling 13, 24–5, 26, 81–2, 107
  teaching 3, 4, 5–6, 20–31, 35–7, 39, 43–7, 57–8, 61–2, 65, 68–71, 72–3, 83–4, 85, 89, 92, 94, 108, 121, 135, 136, 137, 138–44
  technology 1, 3, 5, 21, 23, 36, 37–42, 47, 49, 59, 79–80
  transformation 6, 21, 143–4
  writing 3, 85–92

"Lived Experience of a Black Man, The" (Fanon) 99
Lolita (Nabokov) 30–1
Lord, Phil 68–9, 71
Los Angeles Times 80, 112
Loyola University, New Orleans 21–2, 23, 32, 35, 62, 68–71, 79, 108, 136, 138–40, 144

McCarthy, Cormac 6–7, 105, 120, 121
McLuhan, Marshall 41
Malady, Matthew J. X. 39–40
Malamud, Randy 134
Mandel, Emily St. John 121
Manguso, Sarah 92
Mann, Michael 33
Marx, Karl 35, 74
Matrix, The (Wachowski sisters) 60
Miami Vice (Mann) 33
Michigan 14–20, 26, 77–8, 101, 104–8, 109, 117–22, 126–7, 132, 133, 144
"Midnight in Dostoevsky" (DeLillo) 37
Miller, Chris 68–9, 71
Mississippi River 7–11, 20–1, 62, 63, 134–5
Modernism 26, 27
Moore, Lorrie 45, 46, 57
Morton, Timothy 70, 109
Movable Feast, A (Hemingway) 46, 47
Mushroom at the End of the World, The (Tsing) 118

Nabokov, Vladimir 30–1
Names, The (DeLillo) 90, 91
National Park to Come, The (Grebowicz) 76, 140
Naturalism 24, 25, 26